DIRECTORY OF SOCIAL CHANGE

A Management Companion

Tim Cook
Guy Braithwaite

Published by
The Directory of Social Change
24 Stephenson Way
London NW1 2DP
Tel: 020 7209 5151, fax: 020 7209 5049
e-mail: info@dsc.org.uk
from whom further copies and a full publications list are available.

The Directory of Social Change is a Registered Charity no. 800517

First published 2000

Copyright © Directory of Social Change 2000

ISBN 1 900360 67 5

British Library Cataloguing in Publication Data
A catalogue record for this book is available from the British Library

Cover designed by Lenn Darroux
Text designed and typeset by Sarah Nicholson
Printed and bound by Antony Rowe, Chippenham

Other Directory of Social Change departments in London:
Courses and Conferences tel: 020 7209 4949
Charity Centre tel: 020 7209 1015
Research tel: 020 7209 4422
Finance and Administration tel: 020 7209 0902

Directory of Social Change Northern Office:
Federation House, Hope Street, Liverpool L1 9BW
Courses and Conferences tel: 0151 708 0117
Research tel: 0151 708 0136

About the authors

Tim Cook began working in the voluntary sector in 1962 and retired in 1998, though he remains actively involved. His last two posts were director of Family Service Units and Clerk of the City Parochial Foundation.

Guy Braithwaite was engaged with communities and voluntary organisations for 40 years and retired in 1990. His last two posts were director of a south London consortium of voluntary organisations and a training officer for NACRO.

CONTENTS

FOREWORD

For over 20 years we have met at least once a month to discuss and reflect upon any matter that was taxing T.C., who throughout that time was director of Family Service Units, then Clerk of the City Parochial Foundation. G.B. would say what struck him about what Tim had said. Out of these meetings developed, for each of us, a wealth of ideas about voluntary organisations, and in particular about those issues which rarely seemed to be addressed in management manuals. The latter did not seem to get to the bottom of our concerns. Not surprisingly, similar themes surfaced time and time again, and we thought it would be both enjoyable for us and of value to others to put our ideas into sufficient order for a wider audience to consider. In doing so we have drawn on both our own and many colleagues' experiences as staff, directors, departmental heads, committee members, Chairs and funders. If there has been one continuous thread it is that, however many management courses are attended, however many rubrics and systems the organisation puts in place, there has to be recognition that people are possessed by feelings and frailties, as well as strengths, which are not readily 'manageable'. They will surprise, delight, bewilder, obstruct or worse. It is the way of thinking about the problems that then arise when people are engaged on a common purpose or a common enterprise that is important. What follows is some of our thinking.

There is one important word of explanation. Whenever we met we always discussed the director's bewilderment, concerns, problems, dilemmas, worries and puzzles. We have never met to celebrate the organisation's success, triumph, achievement, or the manifestly excellent working of the staff team – there was always another time and place for that. But certainly for us in our working lives and for most, if not all, voluntary organisations most of the time, the staff team supported by director and management committee gets on with the job and is not caught up in the kind of turbulence addressed in this book. We have an optimistic view of voluntary sector endeavour – we would soon have stopped meeting if we had not. But we remain alert to and very exercised by how suddenly and unexpectedly, albeit temporarily, organisations can be grounded on one of numerous sandbanks, resulting in considerable anxiety, at the very least, until some kind of refloating is possible.

Acknowledgements

All our colleagues and friends have over the years greatly enriched our work in the voluntary sector as well as our reflections upon it. They are too numerous to mention but we especially wish to thank Alan Cripps, Margaret Granowski, Maurice Harker, Elspeth Kyle, Patrick Logan, Annie Smith, Janet Williams and the whole team at the City Parochial Foundation. We are extremely grateful to Alison Harker, Harry Marsh, Philip Peatfield and John Taylor for their continuing support and friendship and particularly for their help in clarifying many of the issues raised in this book. We would like to thank Sarah Lawson for so readily providing information about Scope.

INTRODUCTION

What is a voluntary organisation?

Voluntary organisation is a loaded term. There seems to be an intrinsic conflict between the two words, yet some element of 'being organised' is unavoidable if people are to work successfully as a group. Most voluntary organisations are small and all the committees are voluntary, so they may feel aggrieved when the staff become unionised or seek more pay. 'We are doing this voluntarily so why should the staff want such good working conditions?'

The notion of just what is a voluntary organisation is endlessly debated by academics, policy-makers and a few practitioners. It is a debate which raged throughout the twentieth century and shows no sign of ceasing. For example, as recently as August 1999 Robert Whelan wrote a report entitled *Involuntary Action: How Voluntary is the 'Voluntary' Sector?* It is not our intention to try and cap the discussion of such reports or attempt a new and workable definition.

Because the vast majority of voluntary organisations are small, the people working in them know what their organisation is and does, and are untroubled by questions of definition. Our working definition of 'small' is an organisation whose staff can comfortably meet together as a whole group, which suggests staff teams of about 12 to 15. Many are of course much smaller than this. We are interested in the small organisations not only because they are in the majority but also because in our experience they are in practice often more complex, not least in the interaction between all the staff and the director.

The issues we seek to address in this book are applicable in many instances to other bodies such as schools or churches, so we would not wish to restrict our terms of reference. Essentially we are passionately concerned with just what is involved in working together. But that voluntary organisations have some distinctive features is undeniable. The following are some of the most significant:

- Voluntary organisations, usually small, are in effect a delicate ecosystem. They are a system of checks and balances, not least between committee and staff or volunteers. Large grants too hastily acquired can, for example, quickly disturb that system.
- Voluntary organisations come into existence to meet need. They are not in the business of creating need. Unlike some commercial enterprises there is no profit motive or easily available measure of success. Needs which the organisations are set up to meet can be intense and very demanding. A sense of being besieged can develop, as demonstrated by, for example, the queues outside the Citizens' Advice Bureau on a Monday morning. A

commercial enterprise would be delighted to see such a queue, but not necessarily a charity.

- How a voluntary organisation has come into existence often explains what it does now. This is especially true when an organisation has been founded by an individual and where the founder is still very much in evidence.
- The committee is a critical feature. The members of it are not required to be knowledgeable about the work of the organisation. They may be recruited through social networks, which can be quite closed. The members have a charitable intent but they are not in need of charity. The committee is a permanent body though its members may change. It exercises ultimate responsibility for the work even though its attention is inevitably part-time.
- Charities have noble purposes and are often there to help 'the poor'. The work can be intense and committees or managers can use 'the poor' or the stated charitable purposes as a reason to demand more and more from staff. Profit cannot be the spur.
- In certain parts of society it is almost a civic duty to be on a committee and people can be on too many of them and never attend. This may lead voluntary organisations to set themselves objectives that they are not in fact geared up to achieve. Committee members do not always think things through and may be mightily relieved when they are able to say, for example, that, 'The vicar has agreed to chair it' – in addition to all his other committees.
- There is always assumed to be a common value base amongst all involved which is rarely made explicit. This contrasts with the profit motive. The value base is often invoked when difficulties occur – 'I thought this was supposed to be a charity' – as a means of resolving the problems as if by an appeal to a higher power.
- Staff have a powerful role in voluntary organisations and it is they who often drive the organisation by putting urgent demands or proposals to the managers or committee rather than the latter seeing themselves as being in the driving seat. This can and does result at times in considerable tension and confusion. This is added to when the users of the voluntary organisation are increasingly expected to play a part in the management of it, and may be pressed upon the committee by the staff.
- The organisations, though having much in common in organisational terms, are frequently highly individualistic. At best voluntary organisations offer extraordinary opportunities to learn and develop for the individuals working with them. Even a small organisation working on a need of national interest will find, for example, that it has opportunities to talk to central government.

- It can be extremely difficult to draw the boundaries of the organisation's activities or of the roles of the people within it. It is easy to become sucked into the work of the organisation, turning up at all hours to 'fix the boiler'. The head of an Oxford college said about her post that 'You should not be too grand to worry about the drains'.
- Voluntary organisations offer a surprising number of opportunities to people who might otherwise never have them, for example employment for refugees or people with learning difficulties.

However defined, there is little doubt that the voluntary sector is part of the national psyche. It was therefore not surprising that when the present government came to power some MPs claimed with pride their voluntary sector credentials.

Mind the gap

It may be that some of the characteristics listed above are unique to the voluntary sector, and that some will be shared with other sorts of organisations, small businesses for example. But almost all will apply in various combinations to voluntary organisations. It is those combinations which demand such careful attention and which we have tried to get to grips with in this book.

A wise and experienced member of Family Service Units' national management committee said to Tim, then director of FSU, that problems invariably occur at the boundaries and in the gaps within an organisation. Over the years we have seen gaps open up in a whole variety of areas.

There clearly need to be gaps: professional distance is the distance which is appropriate. The management committee should not manage on a day-to-day basis. If there is an absence of any such distance then serious organisational problems can well arise: a trustee as the main funder; the Chair being related to the director; the director sharing a house with the Chair. Here the absence of a gap means things are too close for comfort. But far more common are the gaps which suddenly open up in an organisation and to which we frequently refer in the chapters to follow.

The director and the Chair find they do not have a common language ('She has no idea at all about the voluntary sector'). Committee members' experience may be so varied and at variance with the organisation's work that gaps open up both on the committee and between the committee and the staff. Enthusiasm and commitment is found to be far from evenly spread.

There are proper differences between director and staff in terms of responsibility and perspective, but care has to be taken to ensure that gaps do not occur in expectations, comprehension and information which make the differences into barriers.

The physical layout of an office can create gaps between staff: 'those upstairs', 'those on the fourth floor', or 'those at the end of the corridor'. These can be terms of humorous endearment, but experience suggests that they are more likely to acquire a dismissive or disparaging tone. Virtue resides in one place and Vice in another.

All these and more need to be watched particularly by the Chair and the director, who could do a lot worse than undertake their own 'gap audit', with no costly external consultants needed. Gaps can and have to be bridged and we try to show some of the ways of doing that.

Who is this book for?

We argue strongly throughout the book for familiarity as a key to help bridge many of the identified gaps, and so we hope that anyone involved with a voluntary organisation will gain fresh understanding about their workplace by reading this. However, more specifically, we have concentrated our attention on the problems and challenges facing those with significant management responsibilities: in particular the Chair, committee members, director and departmental heads (the last are often in effect 'directors' in their own particular world). We hope that anyone contemplating taking on any of these roles will also find the book illuminating.

The essential emphasis is on relationships, which cannot easily, if at all, be wrapped up in structures and systems. The paramount importance of some relationships, such as that between the Chair and the director, or between the director and the staff team, is self-evident. Other aspects of relationships may not initially be so striking but nonetheless need consideration, so we discuss, for example, the value of courtesy and good manners in the staff team.

It is of course the staff team which essentially undertakes the work for which the charity is known and for which funds are given. Part of any management responsibility is to be sure that the staff are aware of what is going on. Good staff work is there in abundance but its recognition requires that the director be familiar with it. Relationships between the director and the team are therefore critical, even though from time to time staff will see events in the organisation differently from the director or the committee. If the divergence of view is too great or continuous then major difficulties arise. Understanding and working with the varying perspective is essential. Staff may not always feel that their work is properly understood. One Chair was in the habit of ringing the office just after nine o'clock each morning to see if the staff had arrived, and then expressing concern to the director when they hadn't. The staff felt spied upon and, more important, that no account was being taken of the many evenings they worked late or even very late. Diplomacy by the director was needed to soothe the many ruffled feathers. There has to be trust that the staff are about their proper business.

There has to be trust at many levels. One Chair said that the relationship between the Chair and the director was 'the closest thing to marriage, certainly in terms of mutual trust'. The notion of trust brings us back again to relationships and the very particular relationships of the workplace. When one is confronted with a real problem, the phrase 'we are dealing with human beings' ceases to feel like a cliché. The collision between the human and the official in, say, the director can be acute.

> 'I needed to talk to the secretary about her excessive sick leave. I thought carefully about when to do it and avoided her birthday and two days when she had important reports to complete and a dental appointment. Unfortunately this meant that when I talked with her it was the day before she went on leave. The result was she accused me of trying to ruin her holiday and walked out.'

This is just one tiny illustration among hundreds of an important issue. Voluntary organisations have a lot of goodwill going for them, but there has to be a constant awareness of the challenges, problems and tensions within such small organisations or everything can unravel very quickly and to everyone's surprise. Gaps in comprehension, role and function soon appear.

SECTION 1
The committee

'I came into the voluntary sector from the private sector. One of the most fascinating differences is working to a management committee or board of trustees and trying to understand their role. I must say it isn't easy.'

'When I realised that I was on 28 committees I decided to come off them all and start again.'

'We now advise our clients to think very carefully before going on to the committee of any charity; the legal responsibilities are really very onerous.'

The committee's tale

'When a group of us started this charity we had no real idea just what would be involved but after a lot of time and effort it has certainly been most worthwhile. Indeed some of us who started it are, ten years later, still active on the committee. We've got a lot out of it as well as helping a lot of people in need. It's not always been easy finding a Chair but usually one of us has been willing to step into the breach. Getting a treasurer has been even more difficult but we manage. We never thought we'd have so much trouble with staff, who at times seem to come and go at alarming rates. We all give our time voluntarily so it's rather galling not to be able to rely on staff, who are quite well paid. But we battle on.'

THE ROLE OF THE CHAIR

Introduction

All voluntary organisations are legally obliged to have a Chair and there is invariably enormous relief when one has been found and duly elected. There is rarely competition for the post. Given the essential and vital nature of the role it is surprising how varied and wonderful are the routes to becoming the Chair. A few large charities now openly advertise for interested people to apply. Much more common is for the outgoing Chair, a committee member or the director to ring friends and colleagues with a familiar question, 'Do you know anyone who would be interested in being our Chair?' The hint of 'please just suggest anyone' can be palpable. Chairs can be elected unexpectedly at the AGM, press-ganged at a social event or pleaded with on a friendship basis by the director. No one knows whether the route to becoming a Chair is any indicator at all as to how effective the person actually is in that role.

Once in the role, and especially if it is for the first time, little in your past may have prepared you for this complex and demanding role. There is little or no glory in it and indeed it can often be the reverse. 'I didn't think chairing a charity would be quite like this,' has been said more than once and will certainly be said again. Running a large corporate body may not make it any easier to chair your local welfare rights agency with its funding crises, high staff participation, volunteers and volatile committee. Indeed some charities have found the highly successful business man or woman quite unable to chair a voluntary organisation. Skills in one area do not always transfer easily to another.

Yet once in post many Chairs soon develop a commitment to the charity. There is often a moral imperative to stay, particularly when organisations are in difficulties. The Chair and the committee hold the organisation in trust and are the legally responsible body, with occasional quasi-judicial authority in, for example, disciplinary matters. Although they clearly should be distant from the day-to-day concerns (an appropriate gap), they do carry the weight of the organisation. We said to one Chair of a charity, which recently had to close, 'You must feel relieved that the burden is going to pass from you.' He said, 'I feel rather guilty.' He had poured years of endeavour and worry into the organisation but had not been able to prevent its closure. And in similar vein one charity director said, 'It has been easier to change my job than come off the committees of other charities'.

Challenges
Authority

Being Chair does not always confer the authority that the title might suggest or even the textbooks describe. The Chair and the director agree that a new project is needed. When the proposal is put to the committee the latter do not agree. They are nervous of the financial implications and may suggest the closure of another project. The Chair struggles even to get a deferment of the decision. He says to the director that being the Chair is 'an impossible job'.

The Chair cannot in fact ride roughshod over the committee. The whole body holds the legal responsibility and so the members are not the Chair's auxiliaries. The Chair is first among equals. He or she cannot sack the committee members, some of whom may have been elected to the committee by another body. It may be that the degree of authority of the individual is in the end more important than the formal authority of the role. As one committee member said about a very effective Chair, 'Because he has real authority he never has to use it'.

Given the statutory responsibilities of committees and Chairs, and the constraints imposed by what can only be their part-time attention to the matters in hand, which is combined with their theoretical and legal final authority, the following questions have to be addressed.

- How is the work to be done?
- In what style?
- How is a Chair's authority to be used?

Attention

What is the style that should be adopted in order to be a good Chair? Just how much attention should the Chair pay to the work of the organisation? Styles range from 'the ignorant and interfering' to the 'supportive and sufficiently familiar'. On any matter there has to be a judgement as to whether the style should be hands-off or hands-on or hardly any hands at all. It is critical to judge the moment when you should pay more attention to the engine room rather than remain on the bridge. One director bemoaned the fact that 'the Chair is never here, he's only interested in his vintage car'. But how often should a Chair be 'there'? The Chair should not appear to be permanently in the engine room or even to want to be there. Directors can certainly tremble when a new Chair asks for office space within the charity.

But trying to get sufficient information on which to base a judgement about what action to take can itself appear to be interfering or intruding upon the responsibilities of the director. For example, asking for information about staff sick leave can imply covert concern about staff absences and appear intrusive or it can simply be an attempt to establish good employment practice. Much may depend on the previous Chair's style, the history of the organisation, the confidence of the director and the relationship between the Chair and the director. Chairs may find it hard to ask genuinely innocent questions!

Giving attention to anything requires energy. Energy in the voluntary organisation is not evenly distributed. It should be at its peak in the director. But the Chair and committee will be required to act vigorously in their own sphere of authority. Sufficient attention, and with it the acquiring of information, should leave the Chair in a position to say not, 'I did not know about this' but rather, 'We have a problem with X'.

Committee colleagues

As we shall see in the section on committee behaviour, the Chair of a charity can be faced with unexpected and challenging problems from his or her colleagues on the committee. Perhaps no one should be surprised by this, but it remains true that many Chairs after particularly difficult committee meetings express bewilderment or frustration at how the other committee members, or some of them, have behaved over a particular issue. There are two themes which are often allied to these difficulties.

Just as Chairs have arrived at their position by a variety of routes, so have other committee members. Some may be there because of a passionate commitment to the cause of the charity but others may be there as representatives of, say, the local council or of a charity working in the same field. It is common on voluntary organisation committees for people to be wearing several hats, but much depends on whether their hats are left in the cloakroom. If not, as Chair, you can face some unexpected problems in the meeting.

You have to try to give equal weight to the contributions of every committee member, for, in order to ensure the courteous and smooth running of the committee, everyone has to be heard. But in weighing up the differing views on an important issue, do you have to take into account factors other than the legal equality of each member? One Chair always ensured he took into account what he called the 'Richardson' factor, named after an exceptionally unpredictable trustee. There is also a need to balance the respective weight of the old and experienced as against the new and questioning. You hope that the new members will stay the course and carry through the implementation of the decision which they are now advocating. But it may not always be easy to distinguish the new from the anarchic. In reaching any committee decision there will be a lot more going on in your head than simply the weighing up of the respective arguments.

Trust

Many of the relationships within a small voluntary organisation may well ultimately depend upon trust, but nowhere is this more so than in the relationship between the Chair and the director. The traumas for an organisation when that particular relationship breaks down are considerable, or indeed when both leave within a very short period. Trust cannot blossom overnight but, even while it is being developed, the Chair, together with the director, has the responsibility to see that the organisation's work is flourishing. As Chair, you have to decide just how much distance to have between yourself and the director, as you do not wish to take over the running of the organisation. At the same time you should not feel flooded with paper and reports so that you are unable to gain any sense of the organisation's overall direction. You have to feel that you are getting the right amount of information at the right time. But even then, there is the critical question of knowing how to question and challenge the information received. It is difficult to ask 'Is that really true?', for that may be too damaging to the vitally important relationship between you and the director.

But Chairs do have to challenge directors just as directors in their turn have to challenge senior staff. Failure to do so can be catastrophic for an organisation. It may be particularly difficult to do if there is insufficient 'objectivity', which can happen when the Chair is an employee in another similar organisation. Chair and director as peers may sow the seeds of future difficulties. We know of several people who, when appointed as directors to voluntary organisations, had as their first task the delicate problem of drawing to the Chair's attention the existing shaky financial basis of the charity. This had arisen because the Chair had not felt able to challenge the departing director sufficiently strongly. Sensitivity to the feelings of a director may well be appropriate on some issues, but the sound governance of the charity has to have priority and it is that for which the Chair carries particular responsibility.

The nature of the work

Many voluntary organisations are engaged in what can only be described as 'nerve-racking work'. In the demands and expectations that the Chair, together with the committee, may have, consideration has to be given to the nature of the work the organisation is undertaking. Stress, anger and frustration may from time to time be manifest in the staff and the director because of the client pressure on them. A key issue for you as Chair is how much attention to give to the nature of the work and how much allowance to make for it in the overall management of the charity. However stressful the work may be, it is possible to become so oppressed by it that the broader issues are neglected or forgotten.

> Laura is the Chair of an organisation that runs a small hostel for teenage girls leaving care. The government has asked for their response to a recent paper on preventing teenage pregnancy. She phones Liz, the director, to ask if she's put together any thoughts yet, since the deadline for returning the questionnaire is looming and she feels it is important for their voice to be heard. Liz is defensive and irritable. The cleaner is off sick and likely to remain off for at least another three weeks, she's just been told that they need major work done to the heating system to make it safe, and the police have been to see her this morning about an incident involving one of the residents. She feels that Laura doesn't understand the pressures of day-to-day management. Yet Laura's question is legitimate for her role, just as Liz's anxiety is legitimate for hers. The challenge for the Chair is to ensure a balance between the two.

Ways forward
Collaboration and consistency

Running a charity has to be collaborative, with a consistency of action and attitudes throughout. While the energy in the organisation will inevitably be unevenly distributed, the Chair and the committee are obliged vigorously to ensure that the organisation is not unprofitable, negligent or exploitative. Indeed it is their job to see that it is morally and financially stable, which is not the same as being motivated by profit. As with the internal management of the staff team and the various roles within it, so with the relationships between Chair, committee and staff, appropriate collaboration founded on sufficient familiarity is essential. Collaboration here signifies conscious effort so that ideas travel easily between Chair, committee, director and staff and not merely in one direction only, particularly not only from the top downwards. To achieve this requires a consistency of approach which is not affected by a difference of role and function. But as the constituent parts act properly and vigorously within their own spheres there can be awkward gaps, and the Chair in particular needs to pay attention to those.

Governance

Although in the end all authority lies with the committee, in practice they have delegated the day-to-day exercise of that authority to a director, who then has to get on and 'run' the organisation, implicitly trusted by the committee.

So what is there for the committee to do apart from meeting its statutory obligations? Because they cannot give full-time attention to the management of the organisation they should not attempt to do so. What they can and should have is 'the long view' as well as the broader view. As ideas flow between staff and committee, together with reports on work in progress, the committee's task is to cast a sufficiently detached and critical eye over what is proposed, viewed in the context of what has been previously agreed, the aims of the organisation and the wider charitable social world. Energetic scrutiny in fact.

It is in this committed, differently energetic environment, that the role of the Chair is crucial, literally 'at the crux' of the organisation: presiding over meetings of the committee with all that entails in preparation and implementation; initiating new internal groupings, be they work groups or sub-committees, to bring about new initiatives; working hand in hand (but not hand in glove) with the director so that the work goes forward and the gaps of role and function do not become gaps of understanding. And although Chairs should not indulge in crisis management they must be able to manage in a crisis. As was said of Captain Cook when his ship hit the Great Barrier Reef in 1770, they should remain 'composed and unmoved by the circumstances, however dreadful they might appear'.

The Chair and the director

As Chair, you are the mirror image of the director and just as the latter can say to the staff, 'I am the director and this is what is going to happen', so you can say the same to the director. But you require a good sense of when to take action and when not to. Committees and staff can be prone to pushing for action, decision or judgement. Your relationship with the director is the most vital piece of the management jigsaw, and you need to know when to hold your nerve and resist pressure for immediate action.

You need to know when to say, 'I will not be rushed into this' or, 'I will have to deal with this by urgent correspondence'. This requires a clear sense of the committee's confidence in you, which in turn depends upon your own sense of your authority and the working ethos of the committee as a whole.

There has to be proper management distance between the Chair and the director. The trick is finding the right way to bridge that gap, for modern technology can erode it quite dramatically.

> Edward was elected Chair at the AGM. As a successful young businessman, it was hoped he would bring a fresh dynamism to the organisation. Within days Susan, the director, was in receipt of numerous faxes requesting considerable detail about forthcoming committee items as well as various policy proposals about the direction of the organisation. Susan was at that time handling a serious staff crisis and felt unable to provide the information requested by the new Chair, so that the position was soon reached where she was receiving faxes containing the Edward's own proposals and then enquiring why she had not responded to his earlier ones. She felt her only solution was to request an urgent meeting between herself and the Chair in order to determine their method of working together, as her new Chair clearly had different expectations from her previous one.

There are many different ways of working together: meeting half a day a week, fortnightly meetings, producing summaries of action taken during the previous month and regular agendas. What is vital is routine and structure. Otherwise the Chair may request 'ten minutes before the meeting' to discuss a difficult matter that clearly needs more attention than that. At the other extreme, one Chair insisted on the director travelling to meet him each month at his club for a meal and a lengthy discussion of charity business. Staff felt strongly that this was a very poor structure! But an appropriate routine and structure should ensure that the governance of the organisation is not dependent upon the good-natured relationship between Chair and director (though it needs to be that as well) but on something more formal and substantial.

Together the Chair and the director should develop a sense of the organisation's wellbeing. To achieve this it is important to have an understanding of what you as Chair really need to know in order to carry out your role properly, and to state this clearly. Proper financial information is one obvious area of required knowledge. Directors can feel frustrated if the Chair 'seems to want to know everything', but equally Chairs can feel undermined if they sense that information is being kept from them or conversely that they are being overwhelmed with paper.

For the Chair, holding the organisation to its long-term goals is critical. This may be more difficult for a director immersed in daily management, especially when it is highly pressurised work. But as Chair you have the vital role of keeping key matters on the agenda with the question, 'What has happened to …?'. There is, in other words, an energy appropriate to the Chair and an energy appropriate to the director. Obviously these are not the same.

Increasingly there are job descriptions for the Chair as well as other senior officers on the committee, just as there have always been job descriptions for the director. Even if every effort is made to ensure that there is no duplication or confusion, that alone will probably not ensure the effectiveness of the management relationship between Chair and director. In a sense there is an equation which governs that relationship and which has as its component parts energy, distance, familiarity, liking and understanding. Each organisation will need to work out how best to express that equation in its own particular circumstances.

Storms

Organisations can find themselves in considerable difficulty if there is a serious imbalance between the strength of the Chair and that of the director. As Chair, through your close working link with the director, you may begin to reach a judgement that the latter is ineffective and that a change is needed. (The reverse can also happen, of course.) This is a stressful and difficult moment and you should be careful not to rush to judgement. Too often, however, difficult situations are allowed to develop so that action has to be taken in a crisis rather than at a more measured pace. To avoid the crisis it is essential that both you and the committee are on the lookout for any early warning signs. Care has also to be taken to ensure that disgruntled staff are not unfairly influencing you, and that concerns about the director's effectiveness are genuine and represent organisational rather than merely personal concerns.

Early warning signs usually do exist and may in the first instance be quite innocuous: for example, receiving reports too late for the committee meetings. It may be that when you contact the organisation the director's whereabouts are not clear or they are frequently off sick. The difficulty is that it may only be a combination of a number of small signs that herald the storm. Understandably, Chairs and their committees do not like to be worried and may at times be too ready to believe that the organisation is in good health. Certainly, when an organisation has gone through a particularly difficult period, there can be an audible sigh of relief and a general feeling that 'all the storms are now behind us'. It may be then that vigilance is particularly needed.

The function of the Chair

The Chair of a large voluntary organisation said: 'The Chair should recognise that the director is the person "running" the organisation. The job of the committee is to establish strategies and policies, in which tasks it is advised by the director. It should support the director in every other possible way and leave him or her to get on with it. The Chair should ensure that the committee has the relevant skills for the tasks and ensure that they are carried out.' This statement sets out the aspirations and spirit behind the role of the Chair but some more specific illustrations about function are needed.

The Chair:

- presides over the organisation and may well at times be the public representative of it;
- has to have sufficient familiarity with the work of the charity to run committee meetings efficiently;
- manages the relationship with the director;
- sets the ethos and tone for management, requiring, for example, regular and clear progress reports, which among other things will frankly expose any difficulties and explain how they are being tackled;
- should establish an appropriate level of questioning and criticism, which demonstrates the expertise and the interest of the Chair and committee but does not cause offence to the director and their team;
- should not try to second-guess the director's decisions.

But perhaps above all the Chair should ensure that proper praise is given when the director and the team do things well and that sympathy and support is provided when things are going badly. Few things are more discouraging for a director at a committee meeting than for there to be absolutely no comment at all on an important paper into which a lot of time and effort has gone.

Ultimately, the Chair has to have a very good sense of what is important to the organisation and ensure that such matters are discussed in the appropriate place. If you become too locked into distinctions between governance and management, a matter of real concern to the director may not get on to the committee agenda. Directors will vary enormously as to what keeps them awake at night.

Conclusion

The role of the Chair of a charity has probably never been easy. But today it is undoubtedly as difficult and challenging as it has ever been. There is no sign yet that the demands being made upon charities by, for example, the Charity Commission will ease. The Chair, with the committee, has to know and control an organisation which is complex and may even seem to be uncontrollable. They give part-time attention to an intense and full-time business. There are no rule books ready to hand. Yet many Chairs once in post work extremely hard to ensure that the charity's services are maintained through thick and thin. However impossible the post may seem, they do not lightly step aside. They recognise that they are not in the same business as 'the bloodless certainties of management consultancy'. The Chair may well have to be, according to the needs of the moment, a constitutional monarch, a benevolent despot or even a dictator, but, as always, careful judgement is needed as to which role to adopt. The constitutional monarchy model was attractive to one Chair: 'Encourage, warn, advise', but be prepared to dissolve parliament if necessary.

COMMITTEE BEHAVIOUR

Introduction

An effective management committee is essential to the wellbeing of a voluntary organisation. Yet despite everyone's good intentions and at times passionate commitment to the particular charitable cause (or maybe because of them), the governance of the organisation can get into the most terrible mess. An AGM lasts 12 hours and then has to be adjourned. Members leave a committee meeting not agreeing on what in fact was decided about the key issue. The Chair feels she failed to manage the committee at an important meeting. The director and staff feel very frustrated that no decision was made by the committee on what they regarded as a vitally important proposal. A critical meeting is inquorate. As a frustrated senior member of staff once said, 'The committee is more trouble than it's worth; can't we take out a grievance procedure against them?'

Yet committee members often go to a lot of trouble to attend committee meetings. They may have to take time off work, fit it in around family life including complex childcare arrangements, travel long distances, depend on unreliable public transport to get there on time, attend after a very long day at work, be only too aware that they simply never have the time to read all the papers, which in any case never quite seem to reach them in good enough time. Committee chemistry can in every sense be wondrous to behold. We have attended hundreds of committee meetings and no meeting was quite like any other. Just as parents can be bewildered by their children's differences when 'we brought them up exactly the same', so Chairs or directors can be astonished at how different one meeting can be from the last when 'all the matters were presented in just the usual way'. Any charity may only be as good as its last committee meeting.

The minutes of any meeting may then tell a different story. No sooner has a committee reached the point for the approval of the minutes of the previous meeting than a voice is heard: 'The minutes do not record the discussion on the photocopier leases as I recall it.' The meeting can be in real danger of a re-run. Many a director has echoed *Yes, Minister* and said: 'The minutes should be written to reflect what people really would have said had they thought about it!'

Variable though committee meetings may be, both within a charity and from charity to charity, there are underlying issues to which attention should be given.

Some problems and puzzles

Arrival

Prospective committee members are invariably invited either to stand for election at an AGM or to join the committee subject to the approval of the other committee members. There may be many reasons why an individual is approached to join a committee: one hopes it is normally because of the expertise and experience that they can bring to the charity. But very often the person whom an organisation wants to have on their committee is already quite busy, so one of the arguments used to persuade them to go on yet another committee is put as follows, 'There are only six meetings a year and we will not make too many demands on you'. There are two puzzles about this approach. First, it rarely if ever turns out to be true and, what is more, everyone really knows that. Second, and much more important, is the fact that it seems rather strange, given the growing importance of management in the charitable sector, to play down the level of commitment and involvement. One colleague, a management consultant, was invited to join a committee on the above terms and found herself attending over 50 meetings in the first year as the organisation went through a period of enormous crisis.

Paradoxically, the very time when good, questioning committee members are needed most can be when it is the most difficult to recruit them. An organisation in crisis is not an attractive proposition. No one wishes to join a ship that appears to be sinking. 'I had just started as director and was asked to find new committee members. It was impossible until it was clear that the organisation was in good condition. I was glad to have them but I could certainly have done with them sooner.'

Committee members, then, will arrive at their first meeting having been invited, persuaded, nominated, exhorted, bullied, flattered or a combination of any of these. They may not necessarily be sure what their presumed expertise is in the particular situation now facing them and, much more important, they may well find themselves managing important charitable work in the company of, initially at least, a group of strangers. It can often be the case that no one is quite sure what anyone else's expertise and experience actually is. It is rather as if a group of musicians has gathered to play in an orchestra but they are all unclear about who plays what instrument until the moment when each instrument is revealed. Committee members may not readily or easily reveal their strengths, for meetings are not easy places in which to say 'actually I do know something about …'. This is a particularly acute problem for a member who is an organisational management expert. They may well feel powerless to help the organisation, of which they are now an integral part, as it goes through great difficulties.

The members of the committee may be strangers to each other, but it is most likely that all will be known to the director or the Chair and may well have been invited on to the committee by either or both. There may therefore be a sense in which the committee members are friends of the director or Chair and bring with them not necessarily expertise so much as a willingness and readiness to help with the work. They are in effect doing a friend a favour. They can bring with them commitment and innocence: 'I know nothing about accounts but I'm happy to help on the finance committee.' Or, as one new member said supportively to the director, 'I agree with anything you say, pet.'

Shared values

Although individuals may come on to committees because of their particular expertise in, say, financial management, given the nature of the work of most of voluntary organisations it is important that there is a shared value base amongst the committee. This is indeed essential if they are to be effective managers of what can often be, as we have already termed it, 'nerve-racking work'. The very nature of many discussions at committee meetings will touch upon the reason for the charity's existence. There always tends to be a presumption that if people join the management committee of a voluntary organisation, then they must by definition share the values of those running it. This is not always the case and can lead to some surprises, not to mention subsequent management difficulties:

'This is a lot of fuss about a potty little playgroup.'
'Should we really be helping refugees?'

> Ken, the Chair of the Family Centre, had recruited Tony, a new committee member who was recently retired and had been recommended to him as someone looking to do voluntary work. At Tony's first meeting the main item was a staff report on family budgeting and debt counselling. Tony was invited to comment and said somewhat exasperatedly 'the first thing they should all do is stop smoking'. He did not attend any more committee meetings.

This illustrates the gap that can exist between an anxiety to secure new committee members, and ensuring that, as it were, their heart is in the right place.

Just talk

Committees are, or certainly should be, absolutely clear that they carry the ultimate legal and moral responsibility and are the group of people accountable to such bodies as the Charity Commission. However, the weight of this responsibility can induce an unnecessary anxiety so that the committee feels it must always be seen to act. Committees abhor a vacuum. They can become driven to take action, which for some is the main purpose of going to so much trouble to attend the meetings in the first place. Committee members can be heard to say after meetings 'it was all just talk'. But taking action may not be what the committee is there to do and it can lead to such a hands-on approach that the director and staff feel powerless. 'Just talk' may be from time to time exactly what the organisation needs, and a staff group that has little time other than for constantly taking action may well value a management committee where talk, and presumably accompanying thought, is the norm.

Unless a committee is clear about its role it can become very frustrated. It is manifestly not there to rubber-stamp all that the director requests, it is not there to debate everything and second-guess the director, and it is not there to 'run' the organisation which it has delegated to the director and the staff. But it has to be more than solely a talking shop, especially given its public responsibilities. To determine the appropriate and effective role for the committee is the task of the Chair in consultation with the director. Harnessing the balance and enthusiasm of the committee is as important for the Chair as doing the same with the staff team is for the director. The committee has to be aware of sufficient detail so that it will not be surprised by events, but at the same time it has to ensure that it provides the long-term perspective and strategies for the director and staff to work within.

Chemistry

In a later section of this book we shall be discussing small teams and what makes them work to good effect. These, however, are groups of people who work together on a full-time basis with an action-driven agenda. Directors or managers will talk about good teams or the good and bad chemistry of the team. It is worth asking therefore whether a management committee, which may well be the size of a small staff team, can be described as a group or a team or whether it is in fact unique. Committees undoubtedly do have their own chemistry, but it is not always as easy to read as the chemistry of a staff team. The fact that a committee only meets occasionally, is inherently part-time in what it does and is to a large extent dependent on what it is told by the director shapes its chemistry or style.

Getting the right style for the committee is not an easy task, and it is part of the critical role of the Chair to try and achieve it. Committees can react to the material before them by becoming domineering. One director walked out of the meeting and the job when the committee rejected out of hand his carefully prepared proposal for developing the Centre, on the grounds that 'this was not at all what David (the founder) had in mind when he started it'. Directors have described committees as bullying. At the other extreme, the committee can become subservient, which among its other consequences can leave staff feeling that the committee is truly hand in glove with the director and that little they say will make any difference. Neither of these styles is useful, but finding just what is the right approach for the work in hand is not easy.

Individual behaviour

A number of colleagues have said over the years (and we would not exclude ourselves from this): 'I can behave very differently, even badly, on committees and in ways in which I would never behave at work.' Some committee members behave badly or at best inappropriately outside the meetings. For a time we tended to view this as an exaggeration, but now we believe that, whilst it should not be overstated, it can nonetheless cause unnecessary difficulties and confusion. Karen was leaving her first committee meeting as director when one of the committee said to her quietly: 'I want you to know that I did not vote for your appointment.'

There are some individuals who regularly give their apologies for absence but who resolutely resist any attempt to suggest that they should resign from the committee as obviously they are too busy. The Chair may feel that the organisation gains by retaining the 'name' on the notepaper, though this is hard on those members who attend assiduously. Simon almost never attended but read all the minutes and in the letter of apology urged the committee to talk less and get on with opening the hostel! Unfortunately, he was never there to hear the arguments. Simply being on some committees is a feather in the cap and part of some other agenda.

There is the committee member who always attends but often arrives slightly late, then proceeds to compound this by saying: 'I'm sorry to be late, and you may already have dealt with this, but I do wish to raise something on the previous minutes.' There are those who produce bombshells under any other business or, worse, raise a highly controversial matter but follow it by saying that they are sorry but they have to leave early. Some will raise a quite fundamental question of great importance to the organisation's work but which, to ensure effective discussion, should have been raised initially with the Chair before the meeting. Indeed, the person may well preface the remarks by saying: 'I know I should have raised this with you, Chair, before the meeting, but perhaps you won't mind me bringing it up in any case.' As a colleague rather cruelly said, committees can become the 'theatre of the absurd', but fortunately for the wellbeing of the charitable world most do not, though at times they may come close to it. A director, puzzled by the dynamics of the meeting, realised that they were in effect played out beforehand in the 'gents' rather than in the committee room itself.

Directors in particular can be very aware of committee behaviour and the potential for things to go badly wrong. We have yet to meet a director who does not on the day of the committee meeting express apprehension rather than say, 'It's great I've got a committee meeting tonight'. Equally, the morning after the committee meeting directors invariably feel overwhelmed, uncertain, perplexed, though in fairness, when it all goes right, they feel immensely exhilarated. There are perhaps three underlying reasons why individuals feel able to behave the way they do on committees, and we are not here seeking to explain away wildly eccentric behaviour of people who should perhaps never be on committees at all. The three aspects are:

- the part-time nature of the activity
- the freedom from their own place of work or normal activity
- the chance to influence.

Committee members know that there are full-time staff whose job it is to implement committee decisions and to pursue as diligently as possible the work of the organisation. It is certainly not the committee's responsibility to run the organisation and, even if they think there are some aspects of it which are rather poorly run, they do not have the time to step in and do it themselves. They are therefore able to raise matters and take decisions, knowing that as a committee they will not be meeting again for, say, a month or in some cases two or three months. Others, the full-timers, will have to do the work. This is as it should be, but it can lead over-enthusiastic committee members to push through courses of action which may be just one task too many for a busy staff team. After the meeting individual committee members may realise just what they have left on the table for the director and colleagues.

'I was somewhat overwhelmed when at the meeting the committee suddenly proposed and agreed to a special 10th anniversary report and lecture, given that I had just spent time explaining to them all the work involved in the new funding applications. The next day two members rang to say that they were concerned about the number of tasks left for me and the staff. One was just concerned. One offered to use her journalist skills to assist with the report.'

The over-enthusiasm referred to above may well arise because individuals can feel free from the pressures or the stresses of their own work and enjoy the challenge of tackling and bringing influence to bear on quite different matters.

Enjoyment is an important element in this because committee members who are really enjoying the work can make an enormous contribution, even if they occasionally allow their enthusiasm to run away with them. Not only do they feel free from the pressures of their own workplace, they feel free to engage energetically with totally different issues. Although individuals may come on to the committee as experts in particular areas, this does not preclude them from being invited to contribute to the discussion of a totally different area to which previously they might have given relatively little thought. There is no argument for confining individual committee members to their areas of expertise, and the committees would be much the poorer were that to be the case. But there is sometimes a price to be paid for letting committee members roam at will, as it were, over the whole field of the charity's endeavours. A former director once said that he liked to regard his committee members as sheep and that it was his job to keep them in the pen, never allowing more than one loose at any one time. Some of us would have been singularly unsuccessful had we aspired to that.

Itch for detail

Committee members can, out of the blue, take both committee and director down a quite unnecessary byway, demonstrating at the very least an imperfect understanding of their respective roles.

> Ken as director of the hostel was presenting the overall financial position but was asked by one of the committee about the food bill. 'What did you buy?' 'Vegetables.' 'What sort?' 'Broad beans.' 'They're too good for our sort of resident.'

The ghost of nineteenth-century committees concerned lest the orphans were being given too much gruel has not been entirely laid to rest.

Last resort

Committees have to balance being given too much information and being drawn too much into things on the one hand with, on the other, not receiving enough information and therefore being surprised by events. The latter can easily happen over staffing issues when there are serious difficulties within the staff, particularly, say, between the director and one or two other members of staff, though the committee should be familiar with the staff team and not just the director. There can be a tendency for a very serious problem suddenly to be dumped into the lap of the committee.

> Sue was the director of a health advisory project employing three other staff. The team had been together for two years. At the committee meeting Sue reported under any other business that she was having great difficulties with another member of staff. There was fundamental disagreement about the philosophy of the work, they now only communicated in writing and another member of staff said he would leave unless it was all sorted out pretty quickly. This concern had not been raised before as Sue felt she ought to have been able to deal with it on her own. This was now an action of last resort.

But committees, not least because of some of the chemistry we have described above, are not the best places or even the appropriate place to deal with what we might call red-hot issues. Frustrated or angry staff or a director can in effect be saying to the committee, 'What are you going to do about it?'. If there is the danger of a really serious staff breakdown, then some action needs to be taken, but it may not necessarily be most appropriate for the whole committee to consider it or for the challenge to be laid at their door. The staff expectations of the committee play an important part in the effective functioning of both and we shall need to look at this in more detail in a later section.

Ways forward

Information

The committee will be at its best when it is composed of members who really care that the work of the organisation is well done. This, of course, must be accompanied by a recognition that the committee is not there to do the core work. If it does not matter to the committee as a whole or to individual members that the work is well done, there may well be passive membership. The key ingredient to bring about a healthy state of affairs is information. Without the appropriate level of information, which has to be sensitively determined by the Chair and director, the committee can remain ignorant and unfamiliar, with a sense of isolation or detachment. Overcoming that state of affairs is not achieved by bracing addresses to the crew but by taking time to explain, often through papers and reports, how what the committee does matters and where their work and responsibility fits into the whole enterprise.

Without the right level of information the committee cannot be familiar with the work, and without familiarity they cannot be engaged. Engagement is critical, for at no level in the organisation is there any alternative to getting on with the job. For committees this means something different from what it means for the staff. But committee members, however recruited, have strengths to be utilised: conscripted soldiers do fight and win battles.

Engagement

To secure the committee's engagement requires that the members are not only familiar with the work of the organisation but are familiar with each other, at least sufficiently to know the strengths and expertise gathered around the committee table. It is remarkably difficult to function effectively in the committee, especially as a relatively new member, if you are unclear or indeed in total ignorance about your colleagues on the committee. There is every reason why potted histories of committee members should be available for all. The Chair and the director will invariably know just who the committee members are, but can sometimes forget that their knowledge has not been shared with the others. The varied and sometimes mysterious routes of arrival on to a committee should not be compounded by continuing bewilderment.

Committees are by definition only occasionally engaged with the work of the organisation but, when they are, what is required from them is their full-time attention, and indeed this is what they wish to give. Securing this requires careful attention. There are five elements which are worth considering:

- induction
- written material
- victualling
- role of the committee
- chairing of the meeting.

The relief at securing new committee members can often obscure the need to ensure that they know what it is they are actually joining. Full and helpful information about the organisation at the outset should be automatic.

> 'I recently retired as manager of the local bank and have been invited on to a number of charity committees. They varied enormously in what information they gave me. I certainly don't know who some of my committee colleagues are. I would also like to meet the staff team but in one case I was told that "wasn't how things worked".'

Ensuring that the committee papers are well ordered and properly numbered, clearly photocopied, arrive in good time before the meeting, are not hurriedly tabled at the last minute, and are clear as to what they are requiring from the committee provides an immeasurably important starting point for the committee's engagement. The time and energy of committee members is vital to the health of the organisation and the last thing that is needed is constant grumbling about the quality of the papers that they receive. For the director and staff it may be a miracle that the papers were prepared at all but, if the committee's functioning is important, then a priority for the staff must be to do all they can to ensure the committee is engaged.

In the great scheme of things, providing a plentiful supply of coffee and biscuits, or whatever is appropriate, for the committee may seem minor. But rest assured that committee attention can soon wander if the hoped-for cup of coffee never arrives. Individuals may travel quite long distances to get to the committee and for some the mid-morning coffee may in fact be their breakfast – the actual case for one committee member whose early morning train continually failed to provide breakfast. Committee members do not expect lavish hospitality, but they should be properly fed and watered if the tasks they are given to do are to have their full-time attention.

As we have commented earlier, committees vary enormously one from another. Most committee members are also serving on one or two other committees, and it will therefore be important to make clear to them the particular expectations or style of your committee. Members will usually be clear about their formal authority, but may well be unclear as to how in a particular organisation the committee is expected to function. Only when they are clear about that can they be expected to engage constructively. There has to be a clear understanding as to how the committee initiates ideas, provides support and raises critical questions. If it has had a recent history of continuous crisis management, it needs to guard against feeling that it wants the director just to get on and run things.

The Chair presides over the committee and its meetings. Managing the meetings is critical and good preparation for them by the Chair and director essential. Every effort has to be made to ensure that major policy matters do not come up under any other business just as everyone is expecting the meeting to draw to a close. Members will certainly not be engaged if agendas are so managed that too much time and attention is given to the detail, which ought to be the province of the director, and insufficient time to the longer-term view and policy perspective.

'As Chair, I always check two things at the start of each meeting. First, I agree the time of ending the meeting so that if anyone has to leave early they can be given the chance to comment on matters of particular interest to them. Second, I ask for notification of any item under any other business and allocate time to it. Anyone raising a major item is advised that it will go on the agenda of the next meeting.'

Time and energy

When engaged, it is remarkable just how much time and energy committee members are prepared to give to an organisation. It is likely and desirable that more will be required from members than simply attending a monthly or a quarterly meeting of the full committee. Even quite small organisations generate at various times working parties, task groups and permanent sub-committees. It is through these that the energy of the committee members can truly be harnessed. 'Energy is eternal delight', but it is only harnessed through specific tasks which engage the personal skills and interests of the individual member. One way forward is to try and ensure that every committee member is on at least one sub-committee or working group so that there is an area of the organisation with which he or she is particularly familiar. Familiarity breeds respect. The likelihood of capricious judgements and decisions is reduced.

Conclusion

With the above in place, the committee can play to its strengths, though good chairing is at all times crucial. It will know its own skills and interests, it will know its particular role, it will be aware of the strengths and enthusiasms of the director and staff. This can be occasionally reinforced by the committee having their own 'social' events which encourage familiarity and promote relationships between committee colleagues. So in a process of collaboration, with sufficient familiarity, it will be able to fulfil its formal responsibilities. But, equally important, it can behave in such a way that it strengthens the arm of the director and staff to meet the needs for which the charity was established and for which everyone in their varied ways is giving a great deal of time.

CHANGING DIRECTION

Introduction

Outside observers will say that a particular charity has 'really changed' since X became Chair or Y director or indeed both together. Normally this is change for the better though not necessarily so. Voluntary organisations are exhorted to change, to shake off the old paternalistic image, to involve users more, to respond to modern needs, to stop relying on an historic funding base and so on. Distinguished journalists feel able to comment that 'charities have lost their way'. Charities wrestling with new accounting procedures and demands can feel that is change enough without embarking on anything more fundamental. Yet innovation is a much invoked term in the voluntary sector world: 'We are nothing if we are not innovative.' Leaving aside the question of whether innovation in certain fields might actually have a proper limit, the climate is undoubtedly one that seems to urge and welcome change. Specific debates about a millennium strategy or 'our role in the 21st century' further fuel the push for change.

Yet the organisation may well be dealing with nerve-racking pressures from the users (see the queue outside the local advice agency which forms an hour before the office opens), be unsure about its local authority core grant or have key staff vacancies to fill. The committee holds the balance between ensuring the basic work of the organisation is maintained efficiently and effectively and initiating or responding to the pressure for change. They literally hold the charity in trust, they are its guardians and will be handing it on to others. How change is managed is a critical part of that. It is not, however, an easy process to handle, and it often brings sharply into focus the relationship between the committee, the director and the authority of the Chair. This can be an especially difficult process when the committee is simply not aware of the importance of its strategic role, so that too much comes to rest on the director, and the change in direction is never 'owned' by the committee.

Issues that arise

The impetus for change

The drive for change may originate in any number of areas. The source may not affect the ultimate outcome but may affect how the process is handled and how different parts of the organisation may initially be concerned or even threatened by proposed changes.

The pressure to change may come from an external source such as the Charity Commission, the Housing Corporation or a major funding body. This pressure may be entirely appropriate and might well be expressing legal requirements. It could be that the organisation would benefit enormously from the changes being required. However, it may be that the organisation feels that it is 'radical' and already far ahead of the measures now being put to it. Insofar as it is legally possible, it may well wish to resist what is perceived as interference by an outside body; some of the Charity Commission requirements around accountancy procedures have had to battle with just such a response. The Chair and director have to balance the proper delight they may feel in the committee's energetic response with what has legally to be put in place.

A new committee member or a group of them may suggest some important changes. Indeed, it is sometimes only in the very early days as a committee member that you see particular opportunities or need for change. How you raise such issues is tricky, as it is possible for it to be viewed as just wanting to make your mark. However, if the committee members have been appointed for the right reasons and their experience is known to and recognised by the other committee members, then it ought to be possible, and indeed desirable, for suggestions for change to come from such a source. The Chair will have the difficult task of ensuring that the proposal from the new members is not just a spur-of-the-moment whim or wheeze but has real substance. Committee wheezes are not often a good basis for long-term change, but another facet of committee behaviour is to put forward quite ill-thought-out ideas.

A powerful and common drive for change often comes with the appointment of a new director. Indeed, part of the interview process is often to ask candidates what changes they think ought to be introduced into the organisation. It is not always easy to reveal one's hand at the application stage! Care has to be taken to see that there is some congruence between the change that the committee may wish for and the change envisaged by the new director. The director may feel that he or she was appointed to bring in change, but the committee may later respond by saying, 'We didn't think that was what you meant by change!'

Staff pressure for change can be considerable. It can be born out of a very clear analysis of the needs of the client group and the consequent importance for the organisation to change to meet those needs. It can also grow out of a general sense of hopelessness that the organisation is simply ineffective. 'This is a hopeless organisation,' is a phrase that can be heard over the coffee cups without any specification as to quite where the hopelessness lies. Responding to staff feelings about change is very important both for the director and committee. The frontline staff see the needs day by day but may not have the necessary long-term perspective. Just as the committee needs to accept that its new members bring vital perceptions and insights, so may the staff have to accept the same possibility with newly appointed colleagues. This may require some delicate handling by the director if gaps are not soon to open up between the old hands and the new.

Resistance

It is highly unlikely that proposals for change, from whatever source, will not meet some resistance. It is not always easy to anticipate the source of any resistance, and it is certainly not easy to judge just how important it is. Some of it can be extremely difficult to counter and be surprisingly aggressive in tone: 'We'll see who wins this one.'

One of the most difficult barriers to overcome can be where older committee members invoke the wishes or the spirit of the dead founder. Founders, as we shall see in a later chapter, can play an extraordinarily powerful role in the history of voluntary organisations and never more so when others use them as a basis for a particular position. The Princess Diana Memorial Fund has been the most recent and most public example of this, but there are others, equally striking, which have never reached the public domain.

Taking care not to be seen to 'rubbish' the past is vitally important. If the older hands, be they on the committee or on the staff, sense their past endeavours are somehow being consigned to the scrapheap, it is highly unlikely that they are going to become passionate supporters for the changes being proposed. All of us are to some extent prisoners of our time, and the past style of a charity may be as much a reflection of the times in which it took place as a comment upon the qualities or abilities of those involved.

Committees can feel resistant to change when it comes from a staff group which they feel does not have the commitment to the organisation that they, as long-standing and dedicated committee members, have manifestly demonstrated. Staff come and go, the committee members go on for ever. It is true that one comes across more committee members who have served for 20 years than staff who have been employed by the organisation for a similar period of time. It will, however, be the very freshness of the staff and their daily contact with the client group that should give them a weight in the debate that needs to be heeded.

> The Advice Service had been running successfully for many years; Colin, as
> director, always reported to the committee the statistics about the large
> numbers of clients seen by the staff. But a few new staff now argued that
> they should give some time to producing policy papers based on their
> frontline experience and use these to press government to change its
> proposals, especially for example in the area of asylum-seekers. It might even
> be better in the long run for one of the advice workers to reduce her advice
> hours to have time to put the material together. Some of the committee saw
> this as 'campaigning' and were unaware that the Charity Commission had
> expressly allowed such campaigning when it arose out of the direct service
> work of the charity. The case was argued strongly and eventually agreed,
> although two committee members resigned as a consequence.

If an organisation has not suffered any great crisis, it is understandable that the committee may well feel, 'We've done all right so far, so why change?'. But the director and the staff, who are in very regular contact with a wide charitable network, may well realise that the external perception of the organisation is that it is 'stuck', and that if change does not occur then financial support may move elsewhere. Committees need to be made aware of these outside perceptions and of the changes occurring in the particular field with which the organisation is concerned. Some committee members may be aware of this through their own work, but more often than not it is the role of director and staff to put this message across in discussions over change.

Visible change

Much of the change which takes place in an organisation is really only seen by those intimately involved. To the outside world an organisation can appear to have spent considerable time and money on changing direction, but all that will be seen is perhaps a change in the name or a new logo. These can easily be dismissed as cosmetic and the committee criticised for having been so embroiled for so long and coming up with so little.

Rarely in fact are such changes simply cosmetic. More often they represent a major change in thinking and in how the organisation wishes to be seen by the outside world. For example, it is vitally important for those working in the field of disability that the organisation is seen as being **of** disabled people rather than **for** them. Similarly, a name and logo can be changed to project a relevant and up-to-date image of an organisation. In 1994 The Spastics Society, founded in 1952, relaunched itself with a new logo and name, Scope, with the strap line 'For people with Cerebral Palsy'. Both potential users and sponsors had been put off by the term 'spastic', which had become a term of abuse. Scope, chosen from an original list of 450 suggestions, was not an acronym but was intended to convey breadth, depth and diversity, and a range of possibilities for people with disabilities. Such changes, so visible to the outside world, can provide a new impetus and new ways of approaching the work within the organisation which can be of great significance. Scope found, for example, that there was a new optimism and sense of pride in staff and volunteers.

The process

Most people involved in an organisation that undergoes important change would agree that the process was as important as the ultimate outcome. Some issues that the process throws up are therefore worth considering.

Whilst every effort will be made to keep everyone on board during the process of change, some may 'jump ship'. It is hard to avoid this, particularly if the changes have been sorely needed. In any case, staff and committee members cannot stay with an organisation for ever. Moments of critical change are often the opportunity some people have been looking for to leave with dignity. It is rare for this not to happen.

Once the change is under way the committee or indeed the staff may feel bewildered by the speed of the change or by the content of it. It is essential that, whatever changes are eventually agreed, the committee and staff can confidently own those changes and not feel in any sense railroaded into them. The Chair and director need to ensure that the committee and staff are given the time to be involved in the changes and in such a way that they are excited by what is taking place. This will dictate the pace of the change. Staff can be more impatient than the committee, but if the change is to have any lasting effect then the committee cannot be 'rushed to judgement'.

One reason why the process invariably takes longer than anticipated is the desire to involve as many of the component parts of the organisation as possible, as well as relevant outside agencies. It is easy, for example, to ignore junior members of staff or members of the finance committee (who you think will only be concerned with the financial implications of any changes proposed). There are then the users, the vitally important group for whom the changes are ultimately made. Ways of bringing users, or representatives of them, into the debate about change can be exciting and challenging but will undoubtedly take time.

Rushing the process can be disastrous if it leads to a situation where the changes that have apparently been agreed simply do not hold because the committee in particular has not really committed itself with heart and mind to them. Whilst it can be frustrating to take months or even years to bring about really significant change, the value ultimately lies in whether such changes become part of the new blood of the organisation. If they do, then the time taken will be well worthwhile and the next generation of committee members will be extremely grateful for it. It is fair to say that, if any change is to be effective and take root in the organisation, there is no group within it of whom it should be said, 'It is really nothing to do with them'. It is always surprising what people have to contribute when given an opportunity to become engaged in areas which are not normally part of their everyday concerns.

A frequent outcome of an organisation's activities when changing direction is the production of a mission statement and a strategic plan. These have now become part of the common currency of voluntary organisations and a great deal of time and effort goes into them. We would like to comment on them.

The mission statement

Many voluntary organisations today see it as necessary to have a mission statement. The production of such a statement is not automatically associated with any change in the organisation, but in practice it is frequently part of or indeed the culmination of a review of the organisation's activities. The mission statement is a relatively new phenomenon in the voluntary sector and it is worth asking what it is meant to achieve and why it is frequently given so much weight. The mission statement sounds dynamic, thrusting, entrepreneurial and even has a militaristic touch to it rather than, say, a religious one, though staff have on occasion objected to the term 'mission' as it evokes missionaries and religious missions, which are against the spirit of equal opportunities. It gives the impression of strength with a tinge of idealism. It even suggests solutions to problems. So important can they now seem that some organisations even apologise for not having a mission statement, almost as if its absence implies that everyone is confused as to what they are doing. As some organisations have found, calling your statement 'Aims, Objectives and Values' can even be to your credit. The mission statement after all does not replace aims and objectives but simply sharpens them to provide in effect a banner or even a sound-bite. 'Making more of being young' can go on a banner or even on a hoarding.

Part of the purpose of the statement is to rally an organisation or to give it focus, but it can give no clue as to how that should be done, unless it is by shouting. In some way the statement is a shout from the organisation drawing attention to it, rather like the wayside pulpit, which can be clever or, at its worst, make your flesh creep. The statements have become part of a new culture, which may have attractive headlines but leave you unsure as to how the organisation is really functioning. It is said that the statement is a message to funders, 'we know what we are about', but in fact some funders are more concerned about how the organisation is going to get from A to B and are not over-concerned about what is on the banner. For other funders, such as corporate ones, mission statements are everyday currency.

If an organisation wants a mission statement, it should have one, but it should be wary of creating an illusion of good ideas without addressing how they are going to be implemented. Rather like brainstorming ideas and putting them on flipcharts, the process can in a strange way preclude thought, as by definition you do not have time to think. The evangelical tone takes over and the 'how' can become the difficult bit. Once in place the mission statement can become the new orthodoxy. This is fine but it will always need to be reformed. It must not become fossilised. The task of reforming and preventing fossilisation falls to the Chair and director, who then have to say to the committee, 'We ought to be looking at this again'. There is then a new cycle of change.

The strategic plan

Much time and effort is spent by many voluntary organisations on preparing a strategic plan, which is often linked to a business plan, the latter being essentially the financial underpinning of the former. All parts of an organisation can become preoccupied with this plan over a long period of time – a year is certainly not uncommon. It is worth asking four questions:

- Who calls for the plan?
- Who is involved in formulating it?
- Is it implemented?
- How often is it ever looked at again?

The fact that the strategic plan is so often used as a fundraising document raises the question as to whether there is such an ambiguous relationship with funders that it is somehow felt a strategic plan is necessary for the funders rather than for the organisation itself. If, for example, funding were absolutely secure and guaranteed for a five-year period, would the organisation expend so much effort on a strategic plan? It would be wrong to suggest that the organisation should not have a sense of direction or understanding of how it is to progress from A to B. At the same time the immediate response to any internal discussion about development is invariably to decide that what is needed is a strategic plan. The organisation may feel it is somehow lessened without it and, in the present intense funding market, senses that such a plan is essential. Given the acknowledged time and effort spent on any such plan, it is important from the outset to be absolutely clear as to who is calling for it and who will benefit from it.

We have already mentioned the vital importance of everyone in the organisation being involved in the process of change, and nowhere is this more true than in the production of a strategic plan. Once the beautifully bound plan with the organisation's new logo and mission statement appears, it will have a considerable weight in the organisation and can become a constant point of reference. If such a plan is perceived as being handed down from on high, resistance to it or resentment of it is increasingly likely. Even within a very small team the capacity of individuals to continue to do their own thing because they do not feel they have been in any way involved in the new plan should never be underestimated. Committees, on the other hand, may feel that they do not want to be involved and are happy to leave it to the director and staff to come up with the plan, but this is an equally dangerous course of action. The committee has the authority to govern the organisation and cannot easily do that if it simply treats the strategic plan as a committee paper on a par with the proposal to buy new photocopiers.

Some organisations understand totally the critical nature of the process of producing the plan and regard that as far more valuable than the final outcome. The actual implementation of the plan then becomes secondary. There is a gap between the two processes, which must be carefully managed or it can lead to considerable disillusionment: so much effort was expended but 'nothing has really changed'. Alternatively, all may realise that the organisation has gained a great deal from the process but recognise that it should not become 'stuck' with the plan. Organisations pride themselves on their ability to respond to rapidly changing needs by their alertness to new funding opportunities; being wedded to a plan can lock them into a position which quickly becomes out of date.

> 'Our strategic plan is just a guide, as so much is changing out there all the time that we cannot afford to pay too much attention to it.'

Conclusion

Even a cursory glance at the history of almost any voluntary organisation will show a process of change. But change is not always undertaken knowingly and committee minutes do not normally state 'we decided to embark on a period of change'. The process can start from a particular point, such as employing the first member of staff with disabilities or the first black member of staff, which turns out to have far-reaching consequences. Wherever it starts, it is not necessarily obvious that it is taking place and its importance may sometimes only be clear in retrospect. But significant change takes considerable time and energy and that should never be underestimated. It can also involve blood on the carpet – the annual report will refer to 'a year of vigorous debate'. Even when all parts of the organisation recognise that some change is needed, the concept will mean different things to different people. Strategic plans and mission statements are the trappings of change and do not in themselves necessarily represent change. Ultimately, however, for a change of direction to occur someone has to commit first, to take the risk of opening up an area for debate. A new director is often well placed to do that.

chapter ④

SELECTING A NEW DIRECTOR

Introduction

There can be no committee decision as important for the organisation as the appointment of a new director or chief executive. A great deal of thought and effort normally goes into this process and it is rarely without its tension and anxiety. It is probably not possible to pay too much attention to the appointment. Yet it can go wrong. Experienced organisations of any size can find that after six months or so the much heralded new director has departed leaving a trail of havoc, confusion and tears. It is not possible to guarantee getting it right, but the dangers of not doing so are real. As a chief executive of a large commercial company said, 'The day we screw up the people thing, this company is over'. He went on to posit that what is needed is a 'multi-skilled, multi-experienced maverick who is at the same time politically skilled enough to keep people onside'. Given that kind of expectation, it is perhaps not surprising that not all appointments succeed.

Some problems that need addressing
Head-hunters

For larger voluntary organisations, and some smaller ones, the first question that is often raised is whether the charity should use head-hunters to help produce a shortlist of candidates. This is an expensive process, but it can undoubtedly save time and effort for the busy committee, and is common enough in the business world. The question that has to be asked, however, is why the committee should delegate any part of its most essential responsibility. It is after all a process and a decision that many committee members might only be involved in once for any particular organisation – unless of course it goes badly wrong. It might therefore be argued that they are surrendering too much of their authority and knowledge if head-hunters are used. Head-hunting can result in manifestly successful appointments, and the final decision will always rest with the committee – or part of it. But has an opportunity been missed for the committee as a whole to become more familiar with the organisation, the kind of director that is needed, and to feel part of a process which ultimately leads to a huge investment, both financially and in many other ways, by the organisation?

The actual job

As the old director plans to leave or possibly even leaves in a hurry, the committee ideally starts to consider how to appoint a successor, though it is by no means unknown for a committee to say to the outgoing director, 'Just you choose someone like you before you leave'. But more usually the job description will be revisited, as it is certain to change if the outgoing director has been in post for any length of time. But apart from what might be written in a job description, the committee will be asking, 'What did John actually do?' or, 'What were Susan's main tasks?' or many other similar questions. What can soon emerge is that the committee as a whole, with the exception of the Chair, has a very partial understanding of the job of the director. Committee members may well have vast experience of directors in other organisations, but this will not always translate across to this particular organisation. Over the years committee members will probably only have seen a small part of the job and each may have seen a different part. The treasurer will know about the director's financial acumen, while others may know about the policy work or relationships with local authorities.

The Chair will have the responsibility of bringing these differing perceptions together and ensuring that the committee does not set off looking for the wrong kind of animal.

> The committee of the Arts Centre has to recruit a new director to replace William and meets for the first time to consider the process of selection. A few committee members, including the Chair, are very familiar with the Centre's productions and William's creative input. Other members have seen William much more as the person who manages the committee business and surprise the Chair by opening the discussion by saying, 'We want someone who is essentially an administrator like William'. A lengthy debate ensues, with the Chair anxious to ensure that there is not a total misunderstanding of the core creative work of the outgoing director. For, if this persists, it will lead to an appointment which would be a mismatch between what is actually needed and what the committee sees relatively superficially at the monthly meetings.

The Chair has to watch the gap between what the committee thinks the director does and what in fact is done. Familiarity once again becomes important. There is a need to test out just how much the committee members know about the director's work and if necessary refamiliarise them with it. As one distinguished Chair said in the middle of an appointment process, 'You certainly get to know a lot about your fellow committee members in this process'.

Clone

An obvious danger for the committee is to focus their attention on a job description which ideally suits the outgoing director, rather than think afresh and see what the organisation might need in a new era. Such a tendency is likely to be more pronounced if the former director has been regarded as very successful and has been in post for a long period. It is vitally important to remember that the director who is leaving certainly did not arrive fully formed and fashioned. Some older committee members may recall hoped-for potential at the start rather than focus solely on the final realisation of that potential ten years later. The opportunity that new blood presents has to be seized, taking great care to retain that which has proven value from the past. However good a new director may appear to be, it is not helpful for the post-holder or the organisation if the message from the appointing committee is 'everything is up for grabs'. In any event change is likely to come soon enough.

The process of appointment

Depending on the size of the management committee it may not be feasible for them all to be involved in the appointments process. This can mean that a specially selected subcommittee is charged with the task of appointing the new director. In practical terms this works well, as anyone who has been on or interviewed by a committee of 20 can testify. It is important, however, for the selection committee to test out in advance their assumptions about the kind of person they are looking for; hidden assumptions that are revealed at the time of the final interview can be a nightmare for the Chair – and they do occur. The chemistry of the smaller committee can also present difficulties, as it may be a group of people who have never worked closely together before, except in the more general atmosphere of the whole management committee. Lastly, however much they may have delegated power to make the appointment, members of the selection panel should constantly strive to involve other committee members who want to know how it is all proceeding. Every effort needs to be made to achieve what one Chair called 'combining collegiality with efficiency'. Attention to fine detail is crucial, however time-consuming it may be; otherwise gaps will soon appear which may widen later on and impede the work of the new director. Even at the long-list or shortlist stage issues can emerge which once again highlight the different perceptions of the various committee members about the kind of director they wish to have. One of the most common of these is, 'We do not appear to have attracted a very strong field'. This is said before any candidate has even been seen, and may say more about the candidates' difficulties in communicating their skills and enthusiasm in writing than anything else. But rather more importantly, it suggests that at least some of the committee have fantasies about the kind of people 'out there' that they believe the advertisment should have attracted, or have an ideal view of the organisation and its importance. It is almost as if there is a platonic ideal of a director that they had in mind when the process started. They want a leader of tomorrow. Sometimes that image turns out to be correct but more often it does not. It makes no allowance for the fact that the person appointed is likely to be someone with potential for growth rather than already fully formed with all skills finely honed. It is the aptitude and room for development that needs to be teased out as much as anything.

Sooner or later the selection committee has to make a decision about who it will appoint or indeed whether to appoint at all. The final selection process may have involved a one-hour interview or a two-day event or something in between, but there is no way of escaping the need to make a decision. Many other committee decisions can be deferred for weeks if not months, but this is not one of them. Arguments will rage about the validity of interviews, psychometric tests, presentations, role-playing and many other instruments of selection, but, when they are all over, the group charged with the task have only themselves to draw on. At this stage a number of key matters need to be borne in mind.

However experienced the selection committee and however objective the process has been, individuals are left with a strong impression about the various candidates. 'He came across as a really strong manager' is countered by 'I thought even the secretaries would frighten him'. Trying to get to the bottom of these impressions and seeing how valid they are is an essential part of the selection business, not least to be sure that prejudice is ironed out. And at this point the chemistry of the committee becomes critical if a sensible decision is to be made.

Then, as the debate starts to narrow down to one or two candidates, new issues emerge that may need urgent clarification. The committee needs to decide whether it should appoint the best person who emerges or continue to look for the best person possible, who may not actually have emerged from this selection process. Is there a view that the ideal should be sought? The best person to have emerged may still fall short of what the organisation really needs. There has to be agreement that the best decision is not to appoint but to start the process again, but can they face going through 'all this' again?

At this juncture the wearing nature of the whole process can create a move to give in and make an appointment. Holding out against such a move is not easy, but a wrong or ill-judged appointment can cause immense problems for the organisation. Veterans of selection committees will urge 'when in doubt, don't'. Making an appointment because the committee cannot face 'going through it all again' may in fact only mean that that is exactly what they have to do in the coming months. At this stage above all, the Chair has a key role to play.

The role of the Chair

As Chair, your role throughout the selection process is one of immense responsibility. You have to hold everything together and ensure that everyone is kept on board. When you are able to report the final decision, you need to have confidence in that decision so you can communicate that strongly to everyone else including the staff. It is often a process where the real nature of your authority is revealed. Are you going to push for your preferred candidate, or abide by a majority decision, or take the view that readvertisement is necessary? It is likely that you will have to work more closely with the new director than any other committee member. You can least easily walk away if difficulties occur. These factors, however, should not necessarily give you, as Chair, inappropriate influence over the appointment.

Media accounts about the selection procedure for the new director general of the BBC, which were fascinating and frequent during 1999, or for the Royal Opera House in 1998, were very good illustrations of the ambiguity surrounding the power of the Chair in the selection process. There are certainly a number of voluntary organisations whose difficulties in selecting a new director mirror exactly the problems within those public bodies. The Chair can take a very strong line that 'we cannot go through all this again', as if somehow any appointment at all will reflect better on the organisation than no appointment. It may be that the Chair can all too easily anticipate the workload that will fall on them should no appointment be made. This is understandable, but it is only a short-term problem; it is not a basis for a decision about such a long-term investment as a new director.

More problematic still is the situation, which does arise, when the Chair insists on their own preferred candidate in preference to the candidate unanimously supported by all the other members of the selection committee. This is a remarkably difficult position for committee members to find themselves in, but often, for the sake of the organisation and their sense of the implicit power of the Chair, it is the latter's voice which carries the day. When the Chair is a significant public figure whom the organisation has gone to some lengths to draw in, it becomes doubly difficult for other members of the selection committee to hold out against them. The problem is that, at the start of the selection process, no Chair will declare that, come what may, their preferred candidate will win the day. Here there is an unspoken assumption which cannot actually be discussed.

But, however arrived at, the appointment process does not neatly end with a public declaration that the organisation now has a new director. There are further issues to be addressed.

After the appointment is made

Staff anxiety

Many small organisations will seek to involve staff in a variety of ways in this selection process, but finally and rightly the decision rests with the committee, and the rest of the organisation is then informed of the decision. It is almost certain to be a time of great anxiety for staff, though its intensity may depend upon the record of the outgoing director. There are three ways in which committees have usually decided to handle the staff during the selection process:

- ignore the staff entirely
- involve them ambiguously in the process
- involve them clearly.

In the first instance the committee felt strongly that it had the responsibility and authority for making the appointment, which was a difficult enough task without trying to take account of the staff in any way. 'It's just taking democracy too far.' The staff suddenly felt rather alienated from the organisation and took out some of their anger on the new director.

In the second case, which is extremely common, the committee was keen to find a way to engage staff in the process, but did it with considerable confusion and ambiguity. A shortlisted candidate visited the staff team and was told: 'The Chair hasn't said anything about you, though we can if we like give comments about you to him. We aren't happy playing these games but, if there is anything you want to ask us, please do.' When that candidate got the job he found this was one of many ambiguities running through the organisation.

In the third case the committee decided to keep the staff fully informed at every stage of the process, with the Chair meeting them to explain the timetable. Care was taken to ensure that the Chair took appropriate responsibility and not the outgoing director. All the shortlisted candidates met the whole staff team of eight individually and as a group. The Chair said to the staff:

> 'If as a result of your meetings you have any concerns that the selection panel should consider, feed this to me through Anna, the senior worker. I will only bring them to the attention of the panel if there is evidence of a serious mismatch between your views and ours. When an appointment has been made I will see you again and outline the reasons for our choice, but this will be for information only.'

The Chair in effect acknowledged that the staff would be the first to sense the power of the new blood, which might be ultimately exhilarating but initially unnerving, and wanted to be helpful in paving the way for the new director.

The outgoing director

The position of the outgoing director is by no means always straightforward. Some voluntary organisations just assume that when a director goes they really do move on, perhaps only staying on the mailing list to receive the annual report. Others, however, do not share this assumption and potentially fraught situations can soon develop. When a director leaves after many years in post, and especially if they were the founder, the committee starts to feel vulnerable and exposed. This is coupled with a strong sense of loyalty to the outgoing director, and proposals are then made to maintain strong links between the two. There are a number of variations on this.

'Soon after my arrival it was suggested to me by the Chair that my predecessor be put on the committee. I did not have the courage to tell him that this would not meet with universal staff approval, but I did go to some lengths to explain that it would put me in a very difficult position. Fortunately, the suggestion was dropped, but I was surprised that the Chair had not realised the implications of the proposal being made.'

'After I had accepted the post I was told by the Chair that my predecessor was going to be retained in a senior fundraising capacity, primarily because the committee were concerned about the flow of funds and were keen to retain the expertise of my predecessor in this regard. It did not seem sensible or even possible to argue against this decision, but it has certainly not been an easy situation to manage.'

'I understand that the final meeting with the committee and my predecessor was quite emotional and, clearly, the committee did not want to lose Roger. As a consequence the committee agreed there and then that he should have some kind of consultancy role, which they were sure the new director would find helpful, and the details of which were to be left to me to negotiate. The expectations of this arrangement were clearly high on both sides, but I find it impossible to implement and have had to run the risk of appearing to go against the very first instruction I have been given.'

The new director

Just as staff can be unnerved and worried by the new director, so can the director by the existing staff. Everything is new and directors can be 'beside themselves with misery' soon after the appointment. This is a critical period that needs very careful management by the committee and the Chair in particular. If there has been a lengthy and exhausting process of selection, there is a danger of a collective sigh of relief when the director takes up the post. The committee's work has been done. The director may be left to introduce unwelcome changes.

Bronwen was the new director of a project for homeless alcoholics. Her first task was to have to explain to the staff that funding pressures and health authority plans meant that they were now going to move more towards work with drinkers before they became homeless. Prevention was to be the new emphasis.

There may be an unsuccessful internal candidate who proceeds to make the new director's life almost unbearable. The excitement of a wonderful appointment turns to tears.

The director has to find out what is important to the committee. What are their expectations and standards? Are they the same as the previous committee he or she worked to? How much learning is needed in working with and managing this committee? How should they be approached when one or two rather nasty skeletons fall out of the cupboard? The latter can be particularly difficult where financial matters are concerned. 'You do realise, don't you, that we have a huge deficit and redundancies may well be needed?' Several directors to our certain knowledge have had to make this virtually their first communication to their new committee. Flying blind is an apt term to describe the early weeks of some new directors.

For the committee the arrival of a new director is a moment when they can take the opportunity to refamiliarise themselves with the organisation, looking at staff appraisal, the financial health of the organisation, the needs of users, relationships with outside bodies and many other such matters. But, above all, the committee, having made the appointment, needs to show confidence in and provide support for the new director. A process of induction, regular and formal supervision will need to be instituted. The director should be encouraged to share both the good and bad news about what he or she is discovering. How the director is managed by the Chair and committee in those early months may lay the foundation for a very successful time for the organisation.

Conclusion

There is no obvious right way of appointing a new director, certainly not one which can guarantee a successful appointment. After all, the committee is assessing potential and the capacity to grow into the job. As was said to one director, 'We thought you would be a very safe, even boring director, but you have proved to be much more exciting and we are glad of that'. Realistically, the most that you can do is to be as sure as you can that the signs for the future are propitious. But the fact that the process can go badly wrong, that extraordinarily poor appointments can be made and that the travails of a selection committee can provide for the onlooker such vicarious delight, all suggest that it is a process that can ensnare the unwary. There are many gaps through which to fall.

chapter ⑤

USERS ON COMMITTEES

Introduction

In the nineteenth century the committee were the 'masters' and paid close attention to all matters. They worried about the quantities of gruel being given to the orphans. No user should ever ask for more. The orphans were not looked to for ways of improving the queueing system for providing gruel. Over many years, however well intentioned committees were, the recipients of the service provided were primarily passive. They were the people who were 'done good to'. The 1960s saw a significant shift, with questions of user involvement or participation being frequently evoked. Psychiatrists asked just what were the differences between the sane and the insane. Theories of labelling were in the air and, when pushed to extremes, almost paralysed some management committees. Barriers between the helpers and helped began to break down.

The beneficial legacy of all this was that the question of how far the service users should be actively involved in the policy development, planning and management of an organisation never went away and indeed gathered momentum. The growing development of self-help organisations, which by definition are entirely user-based, only served to emphasise even further the importance of the issue. During 1999 the Charity Commission, following consultation, produced its own statement about the legal issues involved in having service users on a management committee. The inherent attractiveness of the idea to many staff involved in voluntary organisations makes it imperative that committees, faced with this development, work to understand the issues involved before embarking upon what is a challenging course of action. Ultimately, there has to be some congruence between the answers to two questions.

- Do users on the committee enhance the management effectiveness of the charity?
- Does it enhance the service delivery to the users?

General involvement

Users can, of course, be involved in organisations, other than simply as recipients of services, in a variety of ways. Being on the management committee may be the apex of such involvement, but it is not the only way or indeed, for some organisations, necessarily the best way. Committee and staff need to give careful thought as to how users can most effectively and productively be involved in the organisation; no one model will fit all voluntary organisations. Tenants of a housing association may be brought into management where they are long-standing users of the housing services provided. This would be a much more difficult way for users who are temporary and short-term, such as in an advice agency. Users may also vary a great deal in the disorder of their lives. Staff and committee will need to consider a large number of factors before determining the particular mechanisms for user involvement which are right for their organisation. Children's charities may initially feel that it is not possible systematically to involve the children. But a few such organisations have used video to record children's views and experiences, which can then be shown formally to the appropriate committee.

Key issues
Preliminary questions

Before any organisation decides to have users on its committee, there will inevitably be a range of questions which it needs to ask of itself. We shall look at some of these. But an important caveat is needed. Committees should be careful not to interview the users in their absence, and should test out assumptions, implicit or explicit, which are being made. For example, committees might feel nervous about having user representation and conclude that, 'We would welcome our clients but they really have too many problems of their own to deal with to want to be involved in management'. Others might assume the users could not find the time to attend or would not understand the nature of the business being discussed. Some of these concerns may be real or mask a fundamental resistance to the concept. Any such assumptions need to be checked against reality, which can more easily be done by beginning with user involvement in some other mechanisms, such as an advisory group or a consultative committee. Care, however, has to be taken not to trap users at that 'lower' level. The Peter Bedford Housing Association, over a two-year period, moved through a formal consultative structure, community meetings, a housing liaison group to two tenants being elected to the council of management.

The first question to ask is whether the committee is embarking upon this process because it is ethically pure to do so. If that is the position, then it is probably, indeed almost certainly, the wrong place to start. Obviously, committees should not behave unethically, but their primary task is to ensure the sound governance of the organisation for which they are legally responsible. There will always be courses of action pressed upon them which may be very attractive, but the decisions the committee makes have fundamentally to be directed towards good and better management.

The committee therefore has to be clear as to the purpose of user membership of the committee, and there should be contained, within that purpose, clear notions of improving both the management of the organisation and the service being delivered to the users. If that element is not strongly present, it is likely that the users are there as tokens of liberalism with little effectively to contribute. Such a token presence may not seriously damage the management, but may have a deleterious effect upon the individual users. That must be avoided at all costs.

It therefore has to be asked whether the users are being pressed into service or whether what is being asked of them is fair. Reluctant users will be no more helpful on a committee than any other reluctant committee member. It is important to ensure that users who are being drawn into this process understand just what is involved. In practice this will invariably mean that the organisation has to devote time and effort to informing and educating users as well as other parts of the organisation such as the staff and committee. It is not a process that can simply be tacked on to existing structures. The organisation may currently have a tone and style at variance with the notion of user representation on the committee. This may reflect the history or the length of time the current staff have been employed or the nature of its funding base or many other factors. But taking account of such factors will be an important part of the balancing act the committee has to maintain.

The risk in questioning whether the proposal is fair to users is that it invites the committee to make assumptions about the users' capacity to understand what is involved in management. But it is right to wrestle with the question, for the present-day responsibilities of committee members of voluntary organisations are considerable. For some people the charitable committee is bread-and-butter work, but for others, and especially for users, the experience may be totally new. Again, this means that resources need to be given to help users gain a clear understanding of what is involved, and time needs to be taken to make the process genuine.

Becoming a user

In the enthusiasm to give users more responsibility for what is happening in the organisation, it is worth just recalling why people may have become users. Many will have a need or a difficulty. They may be referred to an organisation which can help them to tackle that need. They are at that point being invited to be concerned with themselves and to get as much as possible for themselves out of the charity. That way progress, recovery and rehabilitation and a less problematic life lies. As a successful resident of a hostel for homeless alcoholics once said: 'I came here to get sober not for all this responsibility.' He certainly did not feel that he should become involved in any way in committee matters.

But at the same time he had useful and important things to say about the service he was receiving.

There is a distinction to be made in the case of self-help organisations where full control of the charity's governance and management is in the hands of users and/or those who have had experience of the particular problem or illness. Here there is a positive acceptance of responsibility.

Users' concerns

In almost all organisations users will make their concerns known, and the process may range from suggestion boxes in the waiting room, through some kind of user consultative group, to staff listening carefully to angry outbursts from users about the way they regard themselves as having been treated. Sensitive receptionists can collect an amazing amount of information about users' concerns which might never reach the staff in the interview rooms. These concerns can be filtered through the staff to the committee when their significance warrants discussion. This can mean the establishment of a new policy. But the filter is the essential part of the process, because the committee cannot involve itself in every day-to-day issue raised by the users. It is the business of the staff to tackle those concerns and, when a way forward is likely to entail a shift in policy, to put that up to the committee for ratification. In this way practice evolves into policy. For example, a new community centre was open to all, but very quickly staff were told by the older users that they were being made to feel unwelcome by the younger people and that, as they had lived locally all their lives, they felt they should have priority. The staff were able to recommend to the management committee more structured methods of operating which ensured that older users were not inadvertently excluded.

With user representation on the committee, care has to be taken that this filtering process is not undermined. Staff can quickly become confused and feel bypassed. The committee can find itself rapidly drawn into a host of individual concerns. But, if users on the management committee are not there to bring out user concerns, what is their role? Policy-making undoubtedly has to be informed by the problems revealed in day-to-day practice. But the users on the committee may not necessarily be the way to achieve that, for they, like everyone else, should be there to fulfil the overall aims of the organisation.

The committee's role

If properly inducted into their role, all committee members, and not just the users, will understand that they have together the overall responsibility for the organisation and that they are not there simply to press a particular interest or perspective. Naturally, all members have particular interests – it is the balance of those interests that makes a good committee – but their role is to contribute on everything. Users should not be confined to commenting only on service matters, any more than a black member of the committee should feel able only to comment on issues of race.

It is highly likely that users will feel more passionately about the repairs and maintenance service for their flats than the way in which the audit was conducted. But feeling strongly about a particular item on the agenda does not mean that is the limit of your engagement. Users are, together with other committee members, now responsible for the audit.

The committee's functioning

What seems common is that, as users take up their places on the committee, the process highlights other aspects of the committee's functioning. In an earlier section we have discussed at some length committee behaviour and how extraordinarily perplexing that can be. When users become full committee members, the importance of the Chair managing the meeting process itself becomes even more critical. However careful the preparation and planning has been for the involvement of users on the committee, probably nothing can quite prepare someone for their first committee meeting if this is not an area with which they are at all familiar. How well the committee simply carries out and orders its business may now require rather more attention than has been necessary in the past, when all members were so familiar with committee behaviour.

In October 1999 Mencap created a new national assembly with one third of the 50 places going to the learning-disabled. A six-month running-in period was decided upon for the assembly because of the need for all representatives to acquire new skills. During meetings participants use coloured cards to indicate whether they are following the discussion. A yellow card means the discussion is moving too fast, a red card says that they need a break, and a green one means that the debate is proceeding at the right pace.

Thinking about the induction of the user members will almost certainly throw into relief the kind of induction process that has been used in the past. If this was less than adequate, it will now need to be re-examined in the light of the very legitimate and distinctly different requirements of user members.

Users will, in many people's eyes, immediately raise the question of conflict of interest, and this is certainly something to which the Charity Commission gives a great deal of attention. However, in many committees this is nothing new, but it may well have been taken for granted. The committee may need to become clear again about how it handles such conflicts for the protection of its overall governance as well as for the wellbeing of the user members.

Initially, it is likely that users' interests will be very hands-on, and it will be important for the committee to encourage them to raise matters pertaining to their interest while drawing them into policy perspective. It is also necessary to ensure that very particular concerns are not presented which are then generalised into inappropriate policies. As an example from a quite different sector, it is sometimes difficult for parent governors of schools to contribute to the general policy on reading without constantly basing their arguments on their own child's particular experience. The user perspective can bring an exciting dimension to the policy debate, but the danger of over-generalisation from the particular always has to be guarded against. It goes without saying that this can occur without users present. But the force and directness of users' experience expressed in the committee can be extremely powerful. This must not mean, however, that users cannot be challenged. One of the pitfalls highlighted by the Peter Bedford Housing Association was the possibility of allowing users to dictate to the non-users. The rules of engagement need to be clear for all at the outset.

User behaviour

If users are not to be a token presence on the committee, they will want to make their voice heard. It is possible for them to do this too vigorously and at some cost to the effective conduct of the meeting itself. But if they are there as responsible members of the whole governing body, users should not get away with any more than any other committee member. They should not be regarded as a protected species. Equally, it should not be assumed that their views are always right and that they are entitled to dictate on matters within their immediate user experience. This may seem harsh and even a pre-judgement about how users behave on committees. It is, nevertheless, important to raise it, partly because it is too often left unsaid and partly because there have been occasions when users have initially caused such difficulties.

A very interesting example of where difficulties can occur is where the users turn out to be much more unforgiving or punitive than the committee or the staff.

> Bob, the warden of a hostel for homeless alcoholics, was pleased when progress had been made to the extent that two residents were put on to the committee. His satisfaction was short-lived. The residents soon showed themselves to believe in a much tougher eviction policy than anyone else. They didn't want anyone upsetting their hard-won sobriety. Concerns about turning residents out on a cold night were met with 'If you can't stand weather like this, you shouldn't be a homeless alcoholic'.

Conclusion

Few organisations have ever regretted encouraging user involvement, up to and including users on the management committee. Few, however, have achieved it easily or quickly. Most have underestimated the time and effort involved and the implications for many aspects of their work, not least the operation of the committee itself. Organisations will never go back to the long-gone days when users had to be as pliant as possible: you took the gruel that was given to you and were grateful for it. Such a style, which had many variations, demonstrated above all else the distance between the committee and the beneficiaries. This enabled unfounded generalisations, fuelled by ignorance and prejudice, to go unchallenged. The increasing tendency to work more closely with users has one undoubted positive consequence. It has made the 'they' now part of the 'we'. This makes it virtually impossible for committees to base important decisions on untested assumptions about what 'they' may think or do. Staff have always been some check on this but it has never been foolproof. Whatever else users may bring to management committees, they bring a live and visible reminder of what the organisation is there to do.

STARTING A NEW CHARITY

Introduction

As the Charity Commission register shows only too clearly, new charities are being established almost daily. But not all new voluntary organisations register as charities, so there are many more such organisations than we shall probably ever know about.

New needs are perceived or, more often, new and better ways of tackling familiar needs are proposed. And so new organisations are born. The impetus can be intensely personal, often related to one's own children or other family members. It can spring from a more generalised concern: 'We must do something about the Kosovan refugees'. It can be closer to home and demonstrate a concern about the local environment. It may arise from an angry or anguished letter to a national newspaper – a phenomenon unique to this country as the impetus for starting a new charity. Whatever the origins, there is always that first meeting for those interested, often around the kitchen table or in a draughty church hall. Suddenly you go home finding yourself on the steering committee of a new voluntary organisation: 'I knew I should never have said that I knew some people at the Charity Commission' or, 'I should never have referred to my previous fundraising experience'. Someone has agreed to be the Chair 'just in order to get things going' but 'certainly not on a long-term basis'. A treasurer is urgently needed.

A surprising number of such initiatives flourish. In 1999 the first-ever *Directory of Supplementary and Mother-Tongue Schools* was published with over 1000 entries, many of which were of very recent origin. A few may one day become household names. After all, when Mencap began in 1946 it was not front-page news. Voluntary organisations are cited as examples of good citizenship, a civil society, a flourishing local democracy, healthy communities and the sheer delight of being British. Their apparently obvious goodness should not blind us to the issues that such initiatives raise. As the Charity Commission sometimes finds, this is not easy to do, as sensitive toes soon feel they are being trodden on. But the very enthusiasm with which such organisations are started requires us to do all we can to husband it, so that they can flourish and achieve what that very first meeting was so keen to do.

Why a new charity?

Outsiders such as funders or the Charity Commission may ask pertinent questions of those involved in establishing a new charity and may even seek to dissuade them. In practice there is little to prevent a group of committed and interested people forming a new organisation to tackle the problem dear to them. It is that certainty that raises the first problem.

Those involved need to be interested and informed and have a conscientious conviction that there is a need to be met. They need to undertake the difficult task of talking to other people to find out whether something relevant is not in fact already being done. It is not always easy to find out what already exists, but every effort needs to be made to do so. Such 'talking around' should be carried out at the earliest possible stage, otherwise there develops a momentum in the formation of a new organisation which is difficult to halt. There may well be a gap to be filled, but more is required than just believing that it is so. Too much certainty too soon can be a serious problem. 'Nobody knows as well as I do what should happen.' Such a basis can make not only registration with the Charity Commission difficult but also obtaining the necessary funds. All charities have to believe passionately in their cause, but being too blinkered can be a destructive pathway.

Inspiration to institution

Quite quickly the group of friends may find themselves as trustees or management committee members, with all the formal responsibility that entails. The person whose idea it was in the first place – whom we shall call the founder – may feel that the meetings only seem concerned with correspondence from the Charity Commission, Companies House, the tax office or the lawyers drawing up the lease for the small office. The organisation now seems rather like all the others in the field, which was why they felt a new one was needed in the first place. It could be said that the inspiration must become channelled within an institutional framework if it is to be more than just a whim. Individuals can, of course, do their own thing but it is the organisation which provides the platform for permanence and, if the need to be met is real and serious, then permanence is essential. Charismatic founders can certainly find this galling.

Early issues

As the new organisation gets into its stride and sets about the business of providing a service, quite quickly there are likely to be a number of issues which need addressing. Some of these may seem quite inappropriate in the early days, but experience suggests that failure to consider them simply postpones the difficulties. We would like to touch upon some of these.

Routines

It is easy in the early days of a charity, with the enthusiasm rampant, to consider that routines are bureaucratic and against the spirit of the charity. We would argue strongly that this is a mistaken view and that proper routines are the route to a more effective and efficient charity. The first 12 months can pass extremely quickly once the charity has been established. Nothing is more frustrating than to be unsure as to whether there is a full record of the minutes, whether the minutes have been numbered so that easy reference can be made to past decisions, and whether all the papers and reports produced for the committee meetings are readily available. These are just small examples, but an enormous amount of time can be wasted by committee members being unsure as to just when a particular decision was made, if indeed it was made at all. Memories play strange tricks.

If and when staff are appointed, the establishment of routines becomes essential. This is true whether there is only one member of staff or several. Systems for managing and supervising staff, for reporting to the committee or for the supervision system within the staff group itself – all these and more should be put in place from day one. It is easy to stress the informality, and that element should certainly not be lost, but if the work of the charity is important sound management procedures are necessary. Attention is frequently paid to financial systems, as everyone can see what will happen if they are not in place. It is much harder to envisage the problems that might occur if staff supervision systems are absent. But problems that do occur in organisations invariably find the organisational cracks, and it is to reduce this likelihood that routines are required.

Staffing

One of the most critical early decisions that a newly formed charity will take is whether to employ staff, always assuming that funding has been secured. If a grant has been given for the employment of one or two members of staff, there is immediate and justifiable excitement in the committee about this early funding success. But problems may only just be beginning. It is common for the trustees of a newly formed organisation to find themselves faced with a number of unexpected problems once they have raised the money to appoint staff they see as essential to achieve the objects of the charity.

Committee members may well come from a variety of different backgrounds, with very different understandings of how best to recruit staff. Some will argue that the charity should rigorously implement its equal opportunities policy and therefore openly advertise the posts. Others may feel that this is an unnecessary expense and that there are obvious people they know, even on the committee, who would be ideal for the post. Indeed, one or two of the committee members know more about the work than anyone else. It may be that the charity has existed to date through the work of volunteers and that among that group there are some obvious candidates. Irrespective of whether the funder has stipulated the method of recruitment, the committee should start as it means to continue. Appointing people to undertake vitally important work simply through friends and contacts will not ensure the best person is appointed. Moreover, managing a director who was a former committee member and was appointed by their friends on the committee could be extremely difficult as and when serious problems occur, which they will.

But let us say that a director is appointed through open advertisement, which does not, of course, exclude applications from existing committee members or volunteers. A difficulty can frequently arise in the early days with that first member of staff. It is often the case that until that time the charity's work has been carried out by volunteers and committee members. Together they may well have put in a great deal of time and effort, which might have gone on for a year or more. The appointment of a full-time paid member of staff can produce some interesting reactions.

There can be a great sense of relief in the committee, to such an extent that they are in danger of letting go the reins of management and new directors can find themselves at sea, looking for routines and procedures to guide them. On the other hand, where committee members and volunteers have contributed a lot in the early days to the charity's work, there can be high, if not unreal, expectations of a full-time paid member of staff who will now be able to do all that they did and more. After all, they were volunteers and gave their time free. Lurking ambivalence about employing staff at all is not uncommon, even though the committee knows realistically that without full-time staff their dreams cannot be realised. But passionate commitment to a cause does not always lead to rational judgements.

Committees may be surprised about the amount of work there is in the process of appointing a member of staff and in ensuring that there are proper procedures in place for their employment. It is again a question of routines and procedures. The fact that there may only be one member of staff does not make the work any lighter. There are the obvious issues of the contract of employment and conditions of service, and committees may find themselves suddenly having to consider matters such as maternity leave. There will also be a need to ensure that there are appropriate disciplinary and grievance procedures. All this is extremely time-consuming but essential to have in place. As remarked earlier, failure to do so will almost certainly mean that the problem arises; nothing is worse than trying to write the disciplinary procedures in the middle of handling a disciplinary matter. But it happens and rather too often.

The first user

If it is important to have in place systems to help the first member of staff, it is many times more important to ensure that they are in place by the time the charity opens its doors to the first user. Not all charities have clients or users and some may be working more in the community development area, for example. But, whatever the nature of the work, there will be a point at which it can clearly be said 'the work begins'. The thinking, the planning, the training and the dreaming changes significantly when the first person moves into the hostel or the first call is taken on the helpline or the first person comes in for advice or the first young person comes through the youth club doors. It is said that new prisons function very efficiently until the prisoners arrive. The same is true for a new voluntary organisation and its users.

It is essential that procedures are clear as to how the users are to be received and dealt with, that there is the minimum of uncertainty and the maximum of clarity about such matters as record-keeping, report-writing and all the other processes that go with an effective service. No one can be certain about the volume of work the charity will be called upon to undertake. Once the flow of users or demands upon the charity gathers momentum, it becomes far too late to try to institute, say, the basic system of record-keeping. Time devoted to clarifying what it is you need to record is certainly not time wasted. The committee or the funders will have expectations and these should be made clear at the outset. An enormous amount of time can be wasted when six months into the operation reports have to be constructed on inadequate statistical data or indeed on no data at all.

Funding

Although there are many charities which run at very low cost and exist on a shoestring, there are many others for which the constant search for funding is a dominant concern. For the charity which has been newly formed with a clear view about the need to be met, this search is paramount. Without resources it will be difficult to achieve what the committee so desperately hoped for when the idea for the charity was first mooted. But their fundraising needs to be organised and patience is required.

There are a huge number of possible sources of funding and they have to give their money to someone. So why not write to all of them? Working through the alphabetical lists of charitable trusts is not unknown. 'We are down to the letter "T" and have sent out over 800 letters, but so far we have had no replies.' So hundreds of letters are sent out as committee members, fired with the wish to secure funds, go off in all directions, making informal approaches to possible funders or writing at the same time as the Chair is writing. Anxiety about securing the funding can make it difficult for the Chair to harness the committee's energy towards taking a methodical approach that is more likely to be successful. Taking time carefully to target possible sources of funds is essential, which might mean, for example, asking a volunteer to go through the directories of grant-making trusts and recommend 20 relevant trusts to approach.

Whatever else the new charity may do, it should not appoint staff until funding is secure. 'On my first day (2 January) as director I was told that the funding was in fact only short-term and there was no funding secured after 31 March.'

It is equally difficult when in the very early life of the charity a new funding source becomes available which does not entirely match the particular purposes of the new charity. Yet large sums of money seem to be available. There is an understandable tendency to try to fit the work of the charity into the new funding criteria. This can mean that almost before the new organisation has got off the ground it is starting to vary the purpose for which it was established. Even a minor variation can, over time, widen and come to distort the essential aim of the organisation; more well-established charities are used to this dilemma. It requires nerve and patience to hold out against applying for inappropriate funding. But, in dealing with funding matters or with any of the issues mentioned above, the voice that will be the most influential, certainly the one most often listened to, will be that of the founder. It is to the role of the founder that we must now turn.

The founder

The idea for a new charity usually begins with an individual and, if the charity is successfully established, that individual may become the first director, the first Chair or just a committee member. Whichever role they have, their influence on the charity is generally profound but not always trouble-free.

A founder might be quite modest and retiring and decide that they are content with the role of an ordinary committee member. But just how ordinary can that be? In almost any committee discussion the weight of the founder's view is likely to outweigh any other or indeed the combination of all the others. An important decision may not be taken until the founder has expressed their views; indeed it can seem that the founder has an unspoken veto which can make managing the committee business very difficult at times. The influence on the committee is likely to be stronger in the early years and wane with time. Equally, time can give the founder an importance, even a mystique, that makes it increasingly difficult to proceed without their manifest agreement.

A founder may become the Chair of the new organisation. In this case the arguments about the weight of their opinion become even stronger. It can well be appropriate for the founder to be the Chair to help drive the organisation forward and give reality to the original vision. It may, however, mean that for the newly appointed director the relationship between the Chair and the director is rather more sensitive than normal. Certainly, the director will be dealing with a Chair who has an especially vested interest in the success of the charity and may well want to pay close attention to the director's actions.

Even more difficult than the above is when the founder is the first director. This often means that the founder has in effect recruited the committee that will manage their work. Indeed this is often the case. This is an understandable process and it would be a strange founder who put together a committee of people totally unknown to them. The committee is then faced with the challenge of how best to manage the person who inspired and founded the charity. It is an interesting historical question to ask just how far Dr Barnardo was managed.

Within the organisation people will say, or at least think, 'no one is indispensable'. But in the early years founders are in fact often indispensable. It may well be their presence and charisma that has attracted funds, for funders like to fund people as much as organisations. They may be the reason that some staff have joined the organisation. It may well be clearly recognised that without the founder and their distinctive influence and contribution the work of the charity would never have happened at all. In times of particular difficulty the founder may well remind the committee of that fact. Staff, whatever their reasons for joining, may also find that questioning the founder or raising issues about the management of the charity is peculiarly difficult. Committees who are in any case likely to support the director are even more likely to find it difficult to challenge a director who is the founder. It may take time for the committee to realise that the skills involved in starting up a new organisation may be different from those required to manage it on a day-to-day basis.

The daily management is not something that normally appeals to founders, even though they may be required to undertake it as director. What seem to some like necessary routines and procedures appear as unnecessary bureaucracy to the dynamic founder. They have started the charity 'to get something done' and are not happy at having to pay so much attention to record-keeping and the business of the committee. For them the work of the charity is not a job but their life. They have seen too many charities become bogged down by red tape and lose their inspiration, and it is certainly not going to happen to them.

> Eric was chairing the finance committee and carefully taking everyone
> through the current financial position, future prospects, budgeting
> arrangements and the likely timetable for obtaining the new residential
> centre in south London. At this point the founder said: 'Oh, didn't I tell you,
> Eric? I've already bought it.'

Much of this drive to get things done is understandable and in the early years is often beneficial for the charity. The energy has to come from somewhere. The problem is controlling it. What is just as difficult is when the founder's inspiration becomes fossilised and fails to take account of the changing climate, be that manifested through government initiatives, funders' priorities or clients' needs. In the early, heady days, this kind of problem is a long way off, and it would be unrealistic to expect the new committee to anticipate it. But what committees can try to do from the outset is to determine how most appropriately they can manage the founder, though there is probably no harder task. The latter wants their work to continue and for it not to be dependent upon their presence, but this is by no means easy to put into practice. Hence the eventual departure of founders is rarely without pain. Sensitive discussions to elevate them to president are not unknown. They become consultants to the organisation but with remarkably vague remits.

At the other extreme, the influence of founders can persist even after they are dead. Committees have been heard to say, 'What would Harry have done?' or, 'I do not think that Harry would have wanted this to happen'. One committee met with the portrait of the founder looming large on the meeting room wall. Many founders may be extraordinary individuals, charismatic or eccentric, but the work they start invariably needs to be maintained: needs do not go away that easily. But charities need to have some eye to the future for, although they may not realise it, the early patterns of work and management will influence it, nowhere more so than in how the founder is managed.

Conclusion

Embarking upon a new charity is to take on a pioneer role; the language some founders use reflects exactly that pioneer spirit. One director, in the early years of the homelessness agency he established, said 'sometimes we were down to the last loaf of bread'. For a new charity to get off the ground, a pioneering spirit is probably essential, but we have suggested that there are issues that need to be considered at the outset. If founders are not pioneering, the road may be an easier one. Even so, it is probably just as well that founders of new charities are not always fully aware of exactly what lies ahead, otherwise they might never start.

SECTION 2
The director

'In the morning I had to deal with a problem with the drains and in the evening entertain the royal patron. This job certainly has variety.'

'Fortunately, although I broke my arm in the evening I was able to get to work the next day. I felt it was important that the staff knew they had a director who pulled their weight.'

The director's tale

'I was really thrilled to get the job of director, though friends did warn me that I wouldn't be doing much directing. The first hour was not auspicious. I was told, "You should know that the administrator doesn't talk to the social workers". Later I learned that the book-keeper was averse to using any computer accountancy packages. There was clearly a lot to do, though perhaps not quite what I expected, as I had been appointed partly because of my experience and knowledge of counselling. I have not worked to a committee before so I need to understand all about that; some of the staff say they "interfere too much", though it's hard to find out what that means in practice. The Chair must have a lot of experience of the organisation as he's been in post for nearly 20 years. He has asked me to think about finding a new Chair as he is keen to step down. It seems odd to be invited to find my employer. There is certainly more to this job than I realised.'

chapter ①

THE ROLE OF THE DIRECTOR

Introduction

Directors, co-ordinators, chief executives – the title may vary but the role is essentially the same, and it is one whose effective functioning is critical to the health of a voluntary organisation. For many directors the post will contain the best of times and the worst of times. Tears of frustration will alternate with whoops of delight and the gamut of emotions in between. Boredom is highly unusual. This will be as much the case in a small organisation with a handful of staff as in a large organisation with hundreds of staff. For new directors it will rarely be quite what you expected, more roller-coaster than plain sailing.

The role is pivotal. The Chair and committee are pleased to have a director in post and want the person to 'run' the organisation. The staff want to get on with their work, may look for a lead from the director and trust them to 'manage' the committee. Funders may see the director as the person with whom they 'can do business'. The director will often be the most public and visible representative of the organisation, yet may not always be sure just how much authority they have in carrying out this function. One director was petitioned by staff not to attend an event at 10 Downing Street as they felt fraternising with government would compromise the organisation, whereas the director saw the event as an opportunity to put the charity on the map, an express part of the director's job description.

Directors make decisions, but how quickly, how often, and after how much consultation? It is important that the director does not appear to vacillate, but equally that their actions do not seem arbitrary so that staff have no idea how and why decisions have been made. Somewhere between those two opposites lies the key to the role, but there is no magic for finding it, just a lot of hard work.

Problems
The last resort

Barbara, an experienced director, was rather surprised to hear the last staff leaving the office even though she could hear an alarm sounding. She later learned that the staff had no idea what this alarm was and just assumed the director would. She in fact took the whole evening to get it sorted out, with the engineers arriving at 10pm. During the evening, as she dealt with the consequences of the alarm, she reflected upon the dilemmas inherent in the role of director. She recalled the head teacher who, as no one else was available, had to sweep up some glass in the school assembly hall and was noticed by one of the pupils, an observant eight-year-old, who asked 'Is that your job, Miss?'

Power and authority

There is an obvious but important distinction to be made between power and authority. Directors do not always heed the difference. Power comes with the post and may well be amplified in the job description. Authority is more elusive and essentially has to be earned. But staff do want directors to have authority and can easily be all at sea if the director does not have it. They can, however, be very adversely affected by the use of power.

The director's job is not for the power-hungry. Describing the post as co-ordinator can be an explicit fudge of the issue of authority. 'Cajoler' might sometimes be a better term! There is without question a lot of responsibility, but just how the authority is to be exercised is sometimes less clear. Authority can become naked power if exercised swiftly and with little or no consultation. Staff recognise the director as having real authority – the organisational chart clearly states that – but may want to feel that such authority is in practice residual. They do not wish to be managed by the brusque memo. On the other hand, staff who are normally resistant to the exercise of robust directorial authority can find themselves requiring it. Interminable delays in making an important decision can demoralise staff and weaken the authority of the director. There may also be situations which call for immediate authoritative action by the director to resolve an issue of great anxiety to the staff. Even benign directors can surprise with an outburst of frustrated authority: 'We will have no more turning up late at staff meetings'. The relationships in an organisation will be greatly affected by the way in which the director handles the authority the role bestows.

Directors are aware that the Chair and the committee entrust them with 'running the organisation', but what does that mean? They remember only too well the series of questions at the interview about their management style, the impressive answers they gave and the obvious belief of the committee that they were the person who could 'run' the organisation. They certainly have responsibility for the health of the whole organisation – quite literally in the above cases of the alarm or sweeping up the glass. Clearly, running the organisation does not mean responsibility for everything, though at times it can seem like that. 'I must confess to being very surprised when Lucy asked to see me for a minute and then proceeded to tell me that there was a lot of mouldy food in the fridge.'

Paradoxically, absolute power may be attributed to the director even though this is not what the person in post feels or indeed wants. A humorous aside over coffee can quickly be translated into the director's plan to take a certain action, producing alarm in the staff. People always assume that the director intends to do something. It almost inevitably goes with the job. No one is ever quite sure how to take a director's humorous remarks. 'Do you think he was being serious?' Directors do come to feel that all eyes are on them. As one head teacher said, 'The joy of retirement is not having to set a good example any more.'

Morale

The director has been entrusted to run the organisation. There is a very full job description which runs to seven pages. But what is not dealt with is how to raise and sustain the morale of the organisation, particularly the staff. A culture of despondency can be remarkably quick to develop and extremely hard to break. A vital element of the role cannot in fact be contained within a list of specific responsibilities or tasks, although these may include words like 'leadership' and 'motivation'. It must almost be taken as read that the director will be responsible for 'this vision thing'.

Any part of the organisation can develop a remarkable capacity to distance itself from it: 'This is a hopeless organisation' or 'This organisation never seems to know what it is doing'. Such comments almost suggest that the organisation is an entity quite independent of staff and committee and ignore the fact that everyone contributes to making an organisation what it is. One director found himself going to more and more outside meetings simply to escape 'life at work'. At the other end of the spectrum, staff can 'look out for' a director they respect and even 'protect' them if necessary. They will not show the same amount of care for someone they do not respect. Directors are often unaware of the care shown by staff – by design.

Directors should not get too far ahead of the team as a whole. They can be engaged in a host of exciting external activities and become extremely enthusiastic about the importance of the work of the organisation. This is clearly healthy, but at the same time they have to watch the gap between their enthusiasm and that of the staff. The director will have more of the 'glory' than any other member of staff, they may well be out of the office more, and they may well be receiving plaudits for achievements that are the work of the whole team. Sharing their enthusiasm with the staff and conveying the vision is astonishingly important. It is part of the constant balancing act between being 'human' and taking the role of director.

Isolation

The director of a small organisation is in effect a lone manager and almost always experiences loneliness and isolation. The work of the organisation is often by definition work where certainty is unusual, as clients' needs are complex and challenging. The director cannot afford to be 'strongly beset by doubt', and indeed the absence of inner doubt is seen as the mark of a strong director. But ways have to be found to express uncertainty and worry about the tasks in hand. It is possible to develop a culture of questioning, for it to be routine: 'I want to hear what you say before any decisions are made'. Being open and willing to change while at the same time not being seen as vulnerable is a balance that needs to be achieved. A director in tears can unnerve staff just as much as a director standing on the table and ranting at the staff. The happy (literally) medium has to be worked at. On occasions directors may have to put on a performance, as the show has to go on and, whatever else they may be responsible for, directors are certainly responsible for that.

The director is likely to feel that they would like to have more support and supervision, but it may not be in the Chair's or committee's understanding or experience that the director needs this, or even what it means. The Chair and committee will be content to handle matters at the monthly meeting and be more than happy to let the director 'run' the business. It may be difficult for the director to express to the Chair, and even more so to the full committee, the nature of the difficulties they are experiencing. There is the proper supervision at the one end, and not being up to the job at the other. But more often than not, organisations are engaged in risky enterprises, and ways have to be found to provide appropriate nourishment for the director. This can come in surprising ways. A director with experience in the private and government sectors said: 'The voluntary sector is the most competitive in which I have ever worked, but I understand why – the prizes for someone in my position are enormous in terms of high profile and public recognition'.

Time

There is never enough time:

'My diary is completely full for the next three weeks.'
'I've been trying to reach you on the phone for days but you are always out at meetings.'
'I know you are busy, but could I just have a minute?'

These and many variations on them are the common currency for directors (and for heads of departments too), and wise directors know that staff who just want a minute in fact require half an hour. There is not even time to go on that time management course that everyone recommends. We all know not to confuse being busy with being effective. But for most directors the sheer range of the tasks that fall to them and the amount of ground they are expected to cover drive them inevitably to acknowledge the confusion without always being able to do a great deal about it.

But, for the director, there is a strong need to have thinking time or a 'still centre' to consider all manner of things, not least a plan or a strategy for the organisation. Worrying about the organisation's future is singularly the director's job. It would be confusing, if not dangerous, if too many of the staff or too many of the committee regularly came up with ideas in this area. They need to respond to the director's plans or vision, and indeed should be required to do so. They also need to understand that time is required for the thinking task, which may not always be an easy one to comprehend. 'I don't know what he's doing in there; he just seems to be sitting and staring out of the window.' It also has to be said that directors can be so overwhelmed that the window-gazing prompts staff to say: 'Do you think Michael is alright? Should we go and see?'

Refill

There are demands on the director to 'give' the whole time:

'Don't worry, we'll sort it out.'
'It's alright, Chair, it's all in hand.'

The physical and emotional demands can be considerable. A good staff team can 'care' for a director and see them through, but even then there is a limit, as not everything can be shared. Finding ways of getting the necessary refill is vitally important; the job of director is not a sprint but a long-distance event. It can often be found in talking on a regular basis to someone who is right outside the job. One colleague said: 'I find ways of breaking out rather than breaking down.'

Making the role work

Unique perspective

Directors need to realise and accept that they have a unique perspective, which does not mean that they are always right, but that they see the whole work of the organisation in a way that no one else can. They are the link between the committee and the staff. Through them all information within the organisation passes, but they have to work to ensure that they are the conduit not a bottleneck. The unique perspective has a number of resonances. It means that the director has a vision of the future and the way the organisation should go. It carries an 'awareness' of everything in the organisation, though the director should not try to know everything. It should also mean that there is a familiarity with the history of the organisation, which can so often determine or influence the way problems are handled or stances taken. This can make the director's position uncomfortable, but it is without question the director's territory.

Working with the Chair

If either the Chair or the director is seriously unhappy in their role, the organisation is in difficulty. It is essential, as we have also seen in the chapter on the role of the Chair, for the director to be clear with the Chair as to the ways in which they will operate together. What is worked out may well only hold for a particular Chair, and new arrangements may have to be made when the Chair changes. Much depends on the personalities of the parties and, for the Chair, on the reasons they took up the post. With each having so much investment in and responsibility for the organisation, time and effort must be put into getting this relationship right.

The director needs to establish with the Chair the following:

■ what amount of information the Chair needs;
■ how much the Chair wants to know;
■ how much the Chair wishes to be advised about;
■ how much is to be discussed before it becomes a paper for the committee.

Above all, they need to have an understanding about what is a policy issue and what are really matters of management. Just because it is an item on the agenda of the committee does not make it policy. In essence, the director needs to have a very clear understanding with the Chair as to just how familiar the latter wishes to be with the operations of the organisation.

Job descriptions for the Chair and the director can be helpful, but some organisations have found that an agreement on the broad remit of the two roles provides a better understanding and more flexibility. Others have found that a director's code of conduct drawn up by a reputable outside body such as the

Association of Chief Executives of National Voluntary Organisations has been helpful and less worrying to their committee. The last thing an organisation needs is a somewhat legalistic dispute between Chair and director as to what really is in each other's job description. The director has to have the confidence to act as a director and has to obtain from the Chair unequivocal agreement that that is what is expected. If the director does not act as director, the Chair soon will.

Working with the committee

Most, if not all, of the committee members will be busy people, some with their own pressurised jobs in the voluntary sector and some giving time from a hectic business world. The last thing they or the director want is to be at committee meetings that are in effect high-level people dealing with low-level matters. Committee members will work to the agenda that they are given, and will not purposely wish to spend their time on minor matters when they must be fully aware of bigger issues that need debate.

Essentially, the director needs to manage the flow of information and matters for decision so that the committee governs rather than manages. Too much care cannot be given to this area of the director's responsibilities. If there is manifestly a major policy issue to be considered, the paper concerning it should not be sent out late or, even worse, tabled – not an unknown phenomenon. Directors should not be Machiavellian and pretend that the paper really only seeks to refine an existing policy! For instance, the director of a grant-making trust may propose that, although the priorities remain the same, it is now proposed to make fewer but larger grants. Whatever the director's view, it would be remarkable if the trustee body did not regard this as a major change requiring the maximum time for consideration. The more the director can give the committee the challenge of tackling the broader issues, the more the committee will seem to be leading rather than to be led. Directors who feel that they are being required to lead on everything may simply not be giving the committee the appropriate level of information and matters for decision. The committee has to have work that matters to them.

It may be that, in very small organisations and at particular moments of difficulty, the director will be extremely grateful that the committee engages in management and is prepared to do so. There could be a funding or staffing crisis that requires much more management by the committee than would normally be the case. This is entirely appropriate, but care needs to be taken to ensure that the committee is not locked into an excessively managerial role.

There are some committees who may be more content to be asked to consider a host of management issues. This may even suit a director who believes that he or she can then get on with the planning and the long-term strategy, for, after all, the director is working on these matters full-time and the committee is only part-time. But there are dangers in this. It ignores the responsibilities of committees as articulated by the Charity Commission. More importantly, it is a short-term view, for the ultimate effectiveness of the organisation will depend on a committee understanding and working at policy issues; a new director would not find it helpful to have a committee which had been kept away from the overall picture.

Since the committee should determine the future of the organisation, if it shifts the emphasis in what the director proposes, he or she should not resent this. But the effective functioning of the committee is dependent on what is put up to it, and in that sense it has to be 'worked'. The relationship between director and committee is like a serious conversation between two people who are not in daily contact but have a common interest in tackling an important problem. The relationship is unequal, as the committee cannot know what the director knows, but they have to say, in response to the director, what 'strikes' them about any item, according to their experience both within and, most valuably, outside the organisation. It may be that nothing strikes the committee at all. This may be because the director has got it absolutely right (a rare event) or that the committee really needs much more time to digest the particular proposal. It is in fact often the case that a few key members were absent and that they were the ones most likely to respond, so they need to be consulted outside the meeting to avoid having to go over the matter again at the next meeting. Keen members do not let sleeping dogs lie.

Working with the staff

Many of the management issues that arise in handling a small staff team are dealt with in the following section, but a few points need to be considered here. As we have seen above, the director's role is extremely varied. It is vital for the director to welcome that variety and not shrink from managing the drains or entertaining the royal patron or everything else in between. The director's territory is in fact often less well protected than that of other staff, who do not switch quite so extravagantly from gore to glory and back again. Many staff may never get any glory at all. But they can and must be drawn into the process of helping the vision (the director's ultimate responsibility) emerge and grow, and derive satisfaction from that. Staff will work with the director way beyond their job description if they are enabled to contribute to and share in the more exciting part of the organisation's work. 'It's not in my job description' can become 'we all work together here'.

The director is the key link between the committee and the staff, indeed is often the only link. The director will work with and see much more of the committee than any of the other staff will. Given the legal responsibility the committee carries, and given the importance of a vibrant committee for the work of the organisation, it is important that the director does not inadvertently undermine the committee to the staff. 'It was a hopeless meeting – they just never decide anything.' The work of the committee should not be a mystery to the staff, and the director can, for example:

- go through the committee agenda with the staff;
- explain to staff how all their work feeds into the committee and can affect the quality of the meeting;
- emphasise that inaccurate financial figures cause irritation;
- show how unclear recommendations delay decisions;
- demonstrate that poorly photocopied or wrongly stapled papers cause confusion;
- after the meeting summarise the discussion and decisions taken.

Directors inherit staff teams, and establishing the style of management in the early days is crucial. The director may find that the staff have not been managed and have no wish to be, although they have no clear idea as to what good management actually means. As one new director said, 'I asked the social worker where she was going and she replied "I don't ask you where you're going, so don't you ask me."' Arduous and draining though it is, such matters need to be tackled at the outset. They cannot be left to fester.

> Janet had recently taken up the post of director of the Women's Health Project. She soon realised that one of the two administrative staff was frequently off sick on Mondays. Nothing was said by other staff, but the looks were telling. She decided to talk to the staff member about her Monday absences. She was taken aback by the reply: 'No one has ever questioned me about this before. Aren't I allowed to be off ill? I thought this project was concerned about women's health.'

The amount of previous mismanagement and misunderstanding that this reveals is enormous, and the director has to show that appropriate management is now in place.

Delegation

All directors know that to avoid a nervous breakdown they must delegate. But having done so, they must not then take the authority away from others. They need to recognise the tasks which naturally 'fall' to the director and those which may be inappropriately 'taken': 'I might just as well do the job myself.' Allowing others to make mistakes is not easy but it is essential. Just as the director wishes to rise to his or her responsibilities, so do others to theirs. One person's pride in the filing system is another's pride in the finely argued submission to the government on its anti-poverty strategy.

When a job has been delegated to another member of the team, the director needs to steer a course between constantly checking to see it is being done and doing nothing in the belief that they should just be left to get on with it. It is possible to provide advice and support, particularly if the task is a difficult one and is stretching the staff member concerned. Members of staff can be seriously dispirited if they have taken on a delegated piece of work but feel unable go back for support at a key stage. It may make all the difference between a job well done and one which will 'simply have to be done again'.

Feedback

Feedback is essential, but it is something that organisations too often do not do well. The absence of feedback is undermining. It is a necessity therefore to create a climate of fair and positive feedback, and the director has an essential role in this. Feedback has to be specific, not general and effusive. Telling everyone they are doing a 'great job' becomes counterproductive. Acknowledging the particular work and worth of others is one of the cementing features in an organisation. Responses to someone's work may be only two lines or a brief word, but they can have a value and significance far beyond that. All parts of the organisation need to know that there is someone 'out there' giving what they do some attention and interest. Spontaneous responses are not naturally part of management, but they can be built into the structure. With positive feedback, staff can spring surprises as to what they can contribute. It is a critical way of developing staff potential. It can help reduce divisions in an organisation, so that people no longer say 'I am only a secretary'. Celebrations of particular pieces of work and leaving parties are good ways of actively recognising jobs well done.

Ironically, directors probably receive less positive feedback than anyone. Such a situation may well go with the job. A head teacher on retirement said: 'I wish that during the past 15 years the staff had said just a few of the very positive things they said to me on my retirement.'

Different styles

Directors should certainly not be arbitrary or wholly unpredictable in their behaviour or decision-making. But they will need a range of styles within their management armoury, which should include not trying to impose themselves on the staff; ultimately, directors only have authority if the staff allow them to have it. (Just as, on a much bigger scale, schools need the consent of the students to run effectively.) Directors cannot afford to give vent to their feelings in the way some of the staff may sometimes feel free to do. At the same time they should not find themselves driven into the position of being the organisation's punchbag. There are times when it is right to say at a staff meeting, with as much force as one can muster, 'We simply cannot go on as we are'. This may produce the reaction, 'We have never seen the director so angry', which may be no bad thing if anger is used sparingly. On other occasions, and ideally more frequently, the director can be encouraging and engage the staff to meet a particular challenge. 'I think if we put our minds to it we can produce a really important contribution to the Government's consultation paper on social exclusion.'

Outside world

The organisation is not an isolated enterprise. It will have numerous relationships with outside bodies, and indeed the director is frequently its representative. The director is 'out and about'. Not all such external activity is exciting or glamorous, but to staff who never leave the office it can appear so. It is important that the director does not neglect 'inside' staff and lets them know where he has been. He needs to bring back the news from 10 Downing Street, as it were. A gap can open up in the organisation when staff start to say that the director is 'never here'. Is he or she up to some good out there?

Priorities

In running the organisation (and no one other than the director can say that this is in their job description), the director has to recognise that they are not only at the head of the organisational chart, but that they are also at the central point through which almost all the transactions of the organisation pass. This can only be handled if priorities are clearly determined, with time being left for the 'still centre' and the appropriate attention to detail. Few things are more difficult than this.

Priorities become virtually impossible to organise if there is in fact simply too much work. The director has to be able to say 'no' to the committee, not least in order to protect the staff, who can quickly feel that the committee has no understanding of what they are doing, as more and more work is piled upon them. Saying 'no' is not something that directors like to do, but, the more the Chair and the committee are truly familiar with the organisation's activities, the more possible it is to say 'no' to good effect.

All one's efforts to create sensible priorities can be thrown off course if the government issues a consultation paper with a terrifyingly tight deadline, which is all too frequently the case. But what can be managed are the internal deadlines where only the organisation itself is affected, and this is an important task for the director. Impossible deadlines are just as harmful as vague ones.

Personal role

When running an organisation, too much attention can be paid to organisational charts, structures, meetings and management texts. And what is often forgotten, particularly in smaller organisations, is the unavoidable personal role of the director. There is a very real place for affection within the various relationships in the organisation. The metaphorical hug can be worth a dozen memos. Whilst everything should not depend on the personality of the director, it is much more likely in a small team that staff will respond to the presence and the person rather than to the job title. If people are only doing the work because 'the boss says so', an opportunity for personal engagement has been missed. Responding to the person not the job title is critical, which means there has to be some understanding of the personal values of the director. Affection and trust come into play, and there can be no more important factors in strengthening the director's role.

Conclusion

The director's position as the conduit, rather than the bottleneck, is a key factor. The constant personal audit for the director is, 'What and where are the gaps, and how can they be bridged, rather than closed?'. You need to broker between the constituent parts and to be the nerve centre in order to ensure that no one is kept in ignorance or feels unfamiliar with other parts of the organisation or the work as a whole. This is an essential element of what you are paid to do. It may not sound very exciting but, carried out effectively, this leads to the freedom to undertake the more challenging or glorious tasks, without which you will only be left to worry about the alarm or the drains. Committee and staff want a director who will put their 'stamp on the matter', and indeed they expect that that will happen. They want the director to be the kind of person who 'commits first', takes appropriate risks and leads the organisation. What they do not want is for this to be done in an overbearing way, which neglects the other parts of the organisation and so fails to safeguard the future. There has to be a balance between activity and restraint.

MANAGING A SMALL TEAM

Introduction

Many directors of voluntary organisations must, if they are honest, envy the Prime Minister when he reshuffles the Cabinet. The lazy, the troublesome, the not-lived-up-to-expectations, the failures or the simply disliked are dismissed or moved sideways. In comes fresh blood and friendly faces. There is no advertising at great cost in the *Guardian*, no danger of industrial tribunals and no agonising selection interview. Fortunately, the voluntary sector cannot work like that (though we know a few directors and Chairs who have tried). Directors of voluntary bodies of all sizes have to grapple with the challenges and problems, and reap the benefits of working in small teams. Here we wish to explore some of the issues lurking in those teams.

We do not, however, have any instructions on team-building exercises. What we wish to do is to bring out the problems that have often perplexed us and that do not always receive much attention in the management manuals. The latter are important, but we suggest that they do not always shed the light you had hoped for.

The notion of the team can be invoked indiscriminately as a mantra or call to action to summon up the blood. But just saying 'we are a team' does not have inherent magic. It can even be destructive, as when a new director began his first meeting with, 'I'm a team player. If you don't want to play on my team, you can go now.' The root of the matter is that a number of otherwise unrelated people are brought together to play their part for a defined purpose. They are 'harnessed in the team'. Should we expect that arrangement to work given that the skills and tasks are various, as are the personalities, and that the team is certain to have a shifting membership? Our experience is that there is a powerful urge to make the concept of the team a reality with a commensurate input of effort.

'Team' implies for us something on a small scale, up to about 15 people, not least because they can be contained in one workplace. Teams and location are inextricably linked. This, incidentally, raises the interesting question of whether it can be a team when some staff are part-time and some full-time or when some work from home. A large charity can have dozens of teams within it. In reality, the vast majority of voluntary organisations are no more than a single small team, and that is the most familiar setting.

Dreams and nightmares

There are few better places to be working than in the team functioning at its best. The phrase 'dream team' is no accident:

'I really enjoy coming to work.'
'I can't wait to get to work in the morning.'
'It's just like a family.'
'This is the best job I've ever had. I don't think I'll ever leave.'

These statements and many others we have heard are real beliefs, based on good team experiences. It is this effective team functioning that all organisations wish to achieve, for without good staff the work will not be done. Fortunately, that is commonly the case, but equally there is a need to be on the look out for the things that can go wrong.

Dreams can turn into nightmares. The dream team can be thoughtlessly wrecked, and very quickly, not least by management by whim. People can become speechless with unhappiness:

'I cry on the way into work every day.'
'I can't bear it. I will have to get pregnant and leave.'
'I will only talk to him if I have to.'
'I'll do my job but that's all.'
'No one can force me to enjoy the work.'
'My divorce was better than this. I never thought working for a charity would be like this.'

These are not imaginary.

Just as politicians talk enthusiastically about family values, so organisations can talk a great deal about team values, without ever being very clear as to what these really are. What is certain is that, when a small team breaks down, it can be an extremely intense and traumatic experience, which everyone would do anything to avoid. It can be extremely difficult, if not impossible, to recover. There is sometimes talk about it being the equivalent of the divorce. Incidents can occur in the team which have all the hallmarks of the kind of situations which arise when people are divorcing or when families are at war. Teams can be in such difficulties that some members always refuse to make coffee for others. Teams can have a familial quality which can be a great bonus but which, when things go wrong, causes immense difficulties and even long-term damage to the organisation. Is it possible to create and maintain the dream and prevent the nightmare?

Seeds of difficulty or even destruction

'A team is only as good as its last team meeting' may be harsh but is worth keeping in mind. We want to look here at what we see as some of the seeds of difficulty, which can lie hidden or be hard to spot even as they shoot forth. Is the apparently innocent question at a team meeting actually innocent or loaded with dynamite?

'Could the director please clarify again the arrangements for the cover of work when someone is off sick?'

Are the healthy now getting fed up with the sick, who in turn say in one guise or another,

'No one can help being sick, I'm not sick deliberately you know'.

But always on Mondays? Or is there a genuine need for clarification? Directors can and do swing between naivety and paranoia, even in the same meeting. Where then might some of the cracks occur in which the seeds can grow?

Creating teams

Even a small team of people can easily contain a huge variety: two staff recruited by you, the new director, one inherited, one in their first job, one longing for retirement, one with a serious health problem, one desperately wanting to leave and so on. This is not an exaggeration.

The good news is that really good teams do occur and we have worked in some and seen and visited many others. The bad news is that there are few prescriptions to produce one. You may inherit a staff in disarray and emerge later with an outstanding team. You may build up a fine team with your own judicious appointments. There are no tricks or obvious routes. Yes, there are bonding weekends, away days, team-building exercises, lectures from successful rugby and cricket captains, but these can do no more than increase the likelihood of creating your dream team. They cannot guarantee it. The team-building, for example, gets off to a difficult start when a senior staff member says in the warm-up introduction: 'I'm only here because I was told to come and I have to leave early.' It is hard to imagine the opening batsman saying the same to the successful cricket captain who is now offering team-building wisdom from the rostrum.

Recruitment

Great care and thought rightly goes into recruiting staff. There are, of course, vitally important procedures such as an equal opportunities policy, which are essential, but it has to be said that luck can play a big part. We all feel it should not but it does. For instance, you may not make an appointment after the first advertisement, as no one seems 'good enough'. A re-advertisement produces some outstanding candidates. Why? No one ever really knows. But it can change the quality of the team. One of the best members of staff one of us appointed was urged by her mother on the day of her interview to leave her sick bed. She staggered to the interview and was appointed. She was a great success, and the history of that team would almost certainly have been very different without her. Staff may leave unexpectedly, though they give their due notice, and suddenly the director is faced with the process of recruitment. Too often the procedures for advertising, shortlisting and interviewing are created in response to the vacancy rather than being in place beforehand. This can create tension and anxiety in the team. Are they all to be involved in every appointment? Are committee members involved in the senior appointments but not the junior ones? Ad hoc groupings of people may be brought together to form the interviewing panel, but they are a group which has never worked together before. Some of this may be inevitable, but it is important for the director to be aware of the issues involved.

Inheriting staff

As a new director, understanding and indeed discovering just who you have inherited is as vital an element as any in creating a team. No behaviour can be too extraordinary for staff who regret the old, dislike the new and are perplexed by notions of change. Organisations may be innovative and challenging but not all members of staff lay claim to that. All inherited staff will be anxious, no matter what the director says. Some will welcome change and see the chance to develop their potential and be listened to, perhaps for the first time. Some may be very obstructive and reduce new directors to tears. Unfortunately, not all such staff always wish to leave: 'You will leave before I do.' With inherited staff the waters can run very deep.

Harnessing talents

The outstanding violinist in the orchestra has ample opportunity to exercise their talents but has constantly to have an ear for the others. The conductor aids that process by harnessing the particular talents. Teams can enjoy having as members individuals with great talent, even basking in the reflected glory, but they do not like prima donnas.

Simply having talented people is not sufficient in itself to make a good team, indeed too many talented people may cause their own difficulties. It is possible for one individual to be too big for the team. There is the not unfamiliar figure of the team member with great experience who does not want the responsibility of being the director, but whose interventions can single-handedly prevent the director exercising their responsibility. This is usually accompanied by, 'I was only saying what I thought' and an expression of surprise that the team has paid so much attention to his 20 years of experience. Working the talents of the team is challenging for the director, but that should be one of their particular talents.

Losing staff

A director of 15 years' standing said to us, 'Every time I build a good team someone leaves'. The better the team and the more the individual's potential has been developed because of that, the more likely it is that the talented people will move on. The director's enthusiastic smile and, 'Of course you must go for that job' is invariably matched by the private sinking heart. Yet the team's reputation may make future recruitment easier. There is the other side of the coin when the person you thought would never leave is offered another job, and your carefully worded reference makes your day. One head teacher went into the stock cupboard and danced with joy when one member of staff told her she was moving on: for that head teacher it was the start of a golden era.

Losing funding

A cruel way of losing staff is through the loss of funding. A frequent response is to create, say, two part-time posts instead of one full-time post. This may be best for the individuals but may have considerable effect on the team and its functioning. There is no easy answer, but we have certainly seen very good teams lose their sense of 'team spirit' when 'make do and mend' staffing arrangements have to be put in place following adverse funding decisions.

Starting again

As indicated, people leave and changes occur in the team, but there is no logical reason why a different team cannot be just as good. No team can be frozen and preserved. When a team has come together it has to be cultivated, but without it becoming set in its ways. It always has to be remembered that the team is not there for its own benefit but for the benefit of others. Directors may well feel that they never have a good team for long enough, but the work that has gone into building one team will stand everybody in good stead the next time. The round of interviews to replace departing staff begins. Everyone who is interviewed will almost certainly be asked whether they enjoy working in a small team. They will all be very positive about this, although it is extremely difficult to assess the truth of any answers given. Efforts have to be made to visualise people in their work, though the only real proof is when the new person starts work in the team. That is where the dangers and the excitement begin again. It can happen that a new member of staff says quite early on, 'I am not a team person'. That raises interesting issues about the nature of a team, which will be looked at later.

Building teams

There are many things that can go wrong in a team and weaken it, though not necessarily destroy it. We have only touched on some that have struck us. Equally, there are some things that can be done that help build and sustain a team.

On arrival

In the early days and weeks of a new director taking up their post there are opportunities for laying the groundwork for team-building. It is very important not to demonise the past, however terrible it might seem to have been. There will still be staff who were part of the past and will not regard all of it as 'bad', indeed may feel a certain loyalty to it. Understanding the history of the organisation in which you are now a newcomer is essential: you should not be imprisoned by it but you do need to have sufficient awareness of it. History's tentacles can be surprising. You need to remember that you are joining an organisation different from the one you left, so that you should not bring with you too much baggage and too many preconceptions about how things work. Setting the tone of your authority early on is invaluable. A senior staff member said of a new director:

> 'It was clear from the outset that he would work as hard as anyone else, not ask us to do jobs he wouldn't do himself and was willing to share information on a very open basis.'

Leadership

Teams have designated leaders, whatever the title (manager, team leader, unit manager, chief executive, director), and their role in building a team is critical. Incidentally, even collectives (leaderless teams) invariably seem to reveal a leader when the situation demands. The director has a unique perspective, and that has been discussed earlier. Part of the stress and strain of the role is the imperative to build a team, to make it more than the sum of its parts.

Building a good team takes hard work over a considerable period of time. The director must have a view of the whole and be alert to tension between one department and another or one individual and another. It is their business to pick up clues at an early enough stage, though this is never easy, as staff are normally very reluctant to pass information to the director about difficulties until they have become either obvious or alarming. The director is in many respects like the conductor of an orchestra, whose members are all expert instrumentalists but who need the conductor to ensure that they retain an ear for each other in order to achieve the best performance of the work.

Vision

Vision and imagination, however hard to measure or even describe, are key elements in ensuring a good team. A team can generate within itself high expectations, and indeed respond to having its expectations constantly raised. Governments issue consultation papers at frequent intervals. The team can develop the expectation that its response to that consultation 'will really make an impact and make ministers sit up and take notice'. That may or may not happen, but the expectation is the critical factor in the life of that team.

Values

Values are an important part of building and maintaining a team. Every organisation has values that are the basis of its ethos. Ideally, all staff know these values, are trained in them and work to them. However, problems can arise when one team has developed its own values, important to itself, but at variance with those of other teams within the organisation. An example of a value clash might be between the advice workers and the accountants. The former may need to have a liberal and relaxed view of procedures as the best way of helping their clients, whereas the latter cannot afford to have any procedures that are in any way lax. It would not do for the accountant to be at all cavalier with regard to the payment of invoices; firm and rigid systyems are required. Whilst such variance in values is understandable and indeed unavoidable, it nonetheless can create problems within an organisation. But, however important the values of a team or a department are to itself, they cannot be allowed to govern a whole organisation. There has to be a limit to the writ of any part of the team.

It is therefore vital in an organisation that departments, even if they are single persons, understand the style and work of the others. People must connect with each other in ways that are appropriate, as the work of the whole organisation relies upon the efficiency of that connection: departments should be 'joined up'. Connecting in this way does not happen spontaneously but has to be worked at. We should not underestimate how hard it is for one department to understand the perspective of another. One department may well say of the other 'surely they knew …'. Departments become very sensitive when they feel that they are not being informed or that they are not understood: 'You do not understand how the finances work.'

Some departments are regarded with more affection than others. The accounts department is almost always unpopular, even though the individuals within it may be well liked. The department responsible for marketing or public relations will see the world differently from frontline welfare workers. The former will want copy that shows the work of the organisation in as dramatic a light as possible, whereas the latter may well wish to avoid publicity and even resent the work of the marketing department. This is probably a legitimate clash of values, but it does not make the building of a good team any easier.

A single department's values cannot dominate the organisation, but the value and importance of new technology can. As organisations strive to become as technologically efficient as possible, divisions can soon occur in a staff team according to their IT literacy. Those who have it acquire more power, whatever their formal position. Those who do not have it express their frustration at the slowness of the service from, say, the one extremely hard-pressed IT manager, who soon becomes a very misunderstood department.

Staff meetings

A common way for people and departments to connect is through the staff meeting. Such a meeting often happens come what may but it can be taken for granted as a mechanism. A lot of attention needs to be given to its management, or even its stage management. We have worked in organisations where it has taken some years to get it right.

The structure and content are vital. The staff meeting should feel more like a Cabinet meeting, not like servants being brought in for prayers and at the receiving end of pious utterances. It is not a vehicle for the director simply to pass on information or, worse, to dominate and harangue. 'We were just told what was happening.' It is a skilled business to manage staff discussion and it needs rules of engagement. The potential for good in the meeting is enormous, but the potential for harm equally so. Intractable problems often start here:

'Three weeks ago I raised this matter and nothing has happened.'
'We are simply never listened to.'

Some staff may be skilful at misusing:

'This may not be the place to raise this but I don't know where else to raise it. It's about reception but it is not personal.'

To a large extent systems and procedures, with a clear process for setting the agenda, chairing the meeting and taking the minutes, can avoid such problems.

Private languages

Language can get in the way of people connecting with each other, even at the staff meeting. Whether the staff are working in or out of the office, it is important, especially in small teams, that they all understand the nature of the organisation's work. It can be too easy to make assumptions about who needs to know what and thereby run the risk of excluding some staff from aspects of the work that they may need to know about, and to which, given the opportunity, they could probably usefully contribute. In a small team it is possible to take the time to engage with everyone whilst taking care not to burden them unnecessarily. Staff will work on the issues and respond to them at their own level. But in full team discussions there is always the danger of jargon entering into the debate and leading to the exclusion of others: some staff do in fact have a private language, and it comes as a surprise to them that all the others are not familiar with it.

Personal experience

The fact that the director may have spent 15 years working on the telephone helpline does not prevent a relatively new worker from saying 'You've no idea what the pressure is like on the help line'. The present experience is invariably seen as different and worse than any past experience. Those providing the frontline services feel under more pressure, and teams start to divide up into the doers and the administrators. Understanding the pressures felt by the receptionist is not easy for those handling the dozens of people coming in for housing benefit advice. This kind of division may be unfair, but teams have to work with it, for it is operationally real.

Gatekeepers

Almost all organisations have within them a department or section which is capable of 'running' the organisation, and invariably in ways which can cause considerable difficulties. A good, if surprising, example of this are the actions of those sometimes referred to as gatekeepers. These can be receptionists, caretakers or telephonists. People in these relatively junior posts can be an immense power for good, but can also cause great difficulties and unhappiness within the team. Directors of voluntary organisations, doctors or head teachers may wonder who exactly is in charge when faced with a person in a gatekeeping post who does not feel part of the team or who has a very different view as to how that team should be working, and to what end.

Receptionists, for example, have to understand why the appointments system is as it is. They cannot just be told about the system and arrangements, for it is their understanding which will enable them to work effectively for the organisation as a whole rather than simply protect their own area of activity. Gatekeepers can cause an organisation to seize up. They can lock the rest out. In creating a good team they are essential, but paradoxically they may well not be central to the enterprise as a whole. A more senior gatekeeper, or in this case 'key holder', is the accountant or company secretary who, because of expertise and almost mystical familiarity with money and markets, can acquire dominance over all parts of the organisation. It is therefore vital that such a post-holder fully absorbs the overall ethos and values of the organisation.

The role of systems

It is tempting for staff, who have been attracted to the voluntary sector for very positive reasons, to view systems or even discussions about systems as creating unnecessary bureaucracy. This was just what they came into a voluntary organisation to avoid. At the same time such staff can be the first to be at risk when an organisation seeks to operate with insufficient or inadequate systems. Like everything else, they have their proper place.

Formalities and routines

Small teams develop a familial quality in which there is often a resistance to procedures: 'There are only four of us, so surely we do not need …'. But formalities and basic structures are an important element in establishing a framework for the activities of the team. It is too often the case that teams end up having to create formal structures when problems arise, rather than having those structures in place to prevent the problems occurring. Routine has its part to play. Team meetings should not be held as and when but every second Tuesday. Supervision too needs routine. No matter how small the team, formalities and routines have a part to play, if only to counterbalance and correct the intensity of the familial and the informal.

Trespassing

Nowhere does the rhetoric of the team break down more quickly than when Bill says: 'I see Harry is opening the post. I thought that was my job.' There are a thousand variations on that theme. Never mind team work, 'trespassers will be prosecuted'. There are situations in which declaiming that 'we are all working as a team' can overcome unfortunate overlaps in job descriptions, but more often we need to pay close attention to properly protected job descriptions. Vulnerability is a highly variable factor in the team, and not everyone is equally able to tolerate trespassers. Directors who have too much to do may well yearn for someone else to take on some of their tasks, but not everyone else welcomes that. At the same time staff should not be pigeon-holed according to job descriptions. If all are to be engaged in the work of the whole team, contributions need to be welcomed from all quarters on all topics:

> 'I wanted to say something about the draft annual report but didn't think I should.'
> 'It really annoys me when after all the work I've done on the draft annual report the secretaries say it isn't clear.'

Neither of these reactions is a healthy one. Trespassers, as it were, should on occasions be made more welcome.

Who's in? Who's out?

Within any team there are those staff whose work confines them to the office and those whose work takes them out all or most of the time. Given the nature of much of the work of small voluntary organisations, this division is not a surprising one. However, it needs watching if it is not to become divisive in terms of the team's functioning. 'They do not know how we have to cope in the office. We never know where they are or when they will be back.' Sentiments such as these can be a common currency in a divided team. Systems need to be in place to ensure that outriders are firmly linked to the base camp. Such systems have to be appropriate and workable. Not knowing leads to suspicion. Working at home is easy for some staff but quite impossible for others, so that some may be seen as having a privileged position because of their greater freedom – although they may work longer hours. Care therefore has to be taken to prevent divisions occurring between the routine workers and the flexible workers, whose job may be seen as not only flexible but also exciting. Everyone has to have a sense of being part of the team, so that they understand the need to maintain regular contact when away from the office. No one should ever be viewed as always or even often absent on mysterious business.

Personal relationships

The intensity of personal relationships in a small team can be very destructive to the work in hand. Yet it is inevitable that in any small group of people, often working on very challenging problems or dealing with demanding clients, there will grow up systems of personal relationships. What is important is to recognise the value of what they can contribute to the work, but at the same time to ensure that such relationships are appropriate to the task. At best they can be of immense value but, like so much else in the team, they need constant attention.

Affection

One undoubtedly creative ingredient in building up a good team is affection, which is not often spoken or written about in this context. We would say that a good team cannot operate without it. It is a strong force and a cementing element. A director needs to show affection liberally and impartially. How this is done will be different for different people, but it implies personal links based on a sufficient degree of familiarity. In this context, familiarity does not breed contempt but rather respect. Affection encompasses enthusiasm from the top, an appreciation of the valuable work done by staff, and courtesy. It means 'giving out' not just hugging people.

Oiling

There has to be a constant oiling of all the parts. Teams do not run on automatic pilot. People do not like to be taken for granted. The word of genuine praise or support is worth a thousand memos.

> 'No one ever told me before that ...'
> 'You're the only person who has commented on the improvements in the reception area' (that from someone who stayed late for two evenings to sort out the reception area).

Sometimes a team needs a semi-official pourer of oil on troubled waters, someone who can soothe ruffled feathers before it becomes a team meeting issue. Having everything out in the open can just as easily produce a blood bath as understanding. The work of truth and reconciliation may well need more time than teams usually have.

Good manners

It may seem quaint to advocate good manners as part of the team's behaviour, but it is surprising how much common courtesies help. Why should a colleague not say 'Good morning'? Shouting at junior staff should not be viewed as 'Well, it's just his way' (it usually is 'his'). Bad manners can reduce people to tears. In *The Times* of 30 July 1998 the junior minister at the Home Office (not an institution renowned for its team spirit) talked of trying to tackle racism in the Office, and part of this was 'about good manners. It's about telling people to exercise a level of sensitivity and respect for their fellow colleagues.' Tackling racism needs a lot more than that but, as in so many other matters, good manners are not at all a bad start.

Work not therapy

What is certain is that the person in charge of the team will be surprised. The surprises can be pleasant or unpleasant. They may find that some staff do not like others. It is not within the power or authority of the director to require staff to like each other. It is obviously better if they do, for strong dislikes can cause serious rifts in any team. But it always needs to be remembered that the workplace is not a therapeutic community. In a good team staff will undoubtedly give a great deal of support to each other when dealing with personal as well as with work problems. That is a sign of an effective and supportive team, but it is quite different from using a team as a platform for trying to bring about change in an individual's personality or way of seeing the world. The director has to set the tone for what is allowed: staff need to be able to call on others for personal support but in the context of recognising that there is work to be done.

More to life

Just as the workplace is not a therapeutic community, so it is not the be-all and end-all of life. Founders, enthusiastic directors, long-serving members of staff may see their work as their life. Not to take a holiday becomes a source of pride. Fortunately, most staff will see work as only part of their life, though they are committed to it when there. Care has to be taken not to have divisions of virtue according to the perceived sense of commitment. Sensitivity to the other demands on team members is vital. Someone who has to leave promptly at five o'clock because of complex child care arrangements is not 'clock-watching'.

Conclusion

Most of the thousands of employees in the voluntary sector work in small teams. People's experiences are as varied as the teams themselves. No team is too small to have serious problems or to be able to achieve great things. Many thousands of users or clients depend on the effectiveness of the team. It is a delusion to say 'No one in the team is talking to each other but the service is not suffering'. The organisation, of which the staff team is a critical part, is there for a purpose. There are numerous and common tell-tale signs of things starting to go wrong, and the director has to be alert to them. Signs may be missed which then combine to produce a real danger.

'I received an e-mail from the advice team complaining that their statistics had been circulated by someone else **and** they have felt for a long time that they "hold the fort" while everyone goes out.'

Getting it right and creating a good team is possible but there are no magic solutions, just some building blocks and a slice of luck. There should not ever be war between staff and director, though there are likely to be small skirmishes with consequent peace treaties. But teams can and do reach a stage where one can say 'They looked upon it and saw that it was good'. Even when, as a director, you know some of that is luck, take some of the credit for it.

SECTION 3
The team

'We used to attend the committee meeting but we stopped going as we just didn't see the point of it.'

'We didn't want to take out a collective grievance against the director, but there seemed no other way to get our concerns heard.'

The team's tale

'We are a small team working hard for what we all believe is a good cause. Some of us have been with the charity a long time and have worked for several very different directors. We use volunteers, though we try not to make the service dependent on them. One or two members of the committee are very well known to us, but others are frankly strangers. We really keep the whole show on the road, indeed we once managed without a director for six months. We know that funding is never easy and our jobs rely on money being raised by the committee each year. But once or twice we've all gone part-time to ease the financial position and we have managed to avoid any redundancies. We certainly do not want the clients to suffer. The Chair once said to us "you're like a big happy family". Funnily enough, that was when we didn't have a director.'

I AM NOT A TEAM PERSON

Introduction

When being interviewed for a post in the team, which can be a departmental team within a large organisation or the whole organisation itself, all candidates will almost always be asked whether they can work in a small team and whether they enjoy doing so. Naturally enough, the answers are positive and in the mind of the candidate totally honest. What is never really explored is whether everyone is meaning the same thing by the notion of team. As we have noted earlier in the book, teams can have a familial intensity, which in practice may not appeal to everyone. A person may therefore be appointed to the post and start work, but may fairly quickly make it clear that they are not gripped by the exhortations to be a team person and will feel able quite openly to state, 'I am not a team person'. Such a statement should not necessarily mean that there is a huge problem, but it certainly requires explanation and understanding if there is not to be a serious breakdown in communication and team functioning.

What lies behind the words?

Just a job

A member of staff is clear that they will do their job to the very best of their ability and undertake the tasks given to them. They appreciate that they should work harmoniously with others in the team and have no intention of being disruptive, spiteful or wilful in any way. Indeed, their references in this regard are excellent. They have pride in their work: 'No one could ever say that I do not do my job properly.' They are genuinely puzzled as to what more can or should be required.

They are certain about one thing: they intend to keep a life outside the office. It seems to them that some of the staff, who have been there quite a long time, have made the work their life and that they have imbibed the spirit of the founder, who gave everything to the organisation. For the new recruit this is not how they wish to go about their work and they do not believe such manifest devotion is necessary to do the job well. It almost seems as if 'team' has come to mean – and this is not unwelcome to the rest – 'everyone knows your business', with the corollary that this is good for the organisation.

Team-building

To the new staff member there appears at times to be almost an 'itch' to have team-building exercises, as if without them the work will suffer and people not work well together. But, for example, the new administrator may have less occasion to be what everyone calls a 'team person' on a day-to-day basis than the three people who are working as the advice team. All staff are asked, even required, to participate in the team-building exercises, but it is clear that not everyone feels as much a part of the team as others do.

Team events are by no means always appealing, and one or two staff can feel out of their depth and seriously inhibited by such exercises. The classroom atmosphere can quickly be evoked as staff are told, 'You all have to say something'. A whole away day is not fun for some people, who can find the event disconcerting, which is not to say that they do not want to work with and have good relationships with colleagues. The team events come to seem as if efforts are being made to capture the 'heart and mind', rather than to help people do their job well. It no longer seems acceptable just to say, 'I am a willing worker'.

Criteria

The importance that everyone, particularly the director, attaches to building up the team spirit through various activities and exercises suggests that staff may well be judged by two criteria. The first of these relates directly to how they carry out their work, and the second implies something about their work, by referring to the quality of their 'team membership'. If the terms for determining the latter are never made explicit, there is a danger that capable staff are as it were 'marked down'. Such staff will feel there has to be an acknowledgement of the difference between a worker who is clearly obstructive and difficult (and will love to spend a day away), and one who is always co-operative and works hard, but who does not wave the team flag in the way that seems to be required. There are tasks to be done, and what is important for some is how they respond week in and week out to the director's cry 'full steam ahead', rather than how they engage or not with team events.

Responses
Team formation

Many of the newer charities will have started with one member of staff, namely the director. That person may or may not be the founder, but will certainly have a founder-like enthusiasm for building up the organisation. For that person there will be a considerable challenge and excitement in the early years. As additional members of the team are recruited, they may or may not share in quite the same way the first director's enthusiasm for the work. Care therefore needs to be taken not to make assumptions about what can be required.

It is probably important to be as explicit as possible about whether staff are just being hired for their skills or whether something more, possibly rather intangible, is expected, even required. Staff may be happy to respond to that extra demand if the expectation has been made clear in the first place; if left unclear it may become a cause for resentment when the director is unable to obtain the desired response. It is here that job descriptions are crucial. These tend to focus almost exclusively on the particular responsibilities of the post, and this clearly has to be the emphasis. But they should also provide the opportunity to make explicit the expectations as a member of the team. It is better to have that in writing rather than to rely on what was said at the interview, now lost in the mists of time.

Judgements

Staff will expect a distinction to be made between those staff who are wilfully disruptive and those who do not find the team spirit very easy to absorb. One voluntary organisation found that the three administrative staff regularly met together over a cup of coffee and formed in effect a protest group, doing all they could to hinder effective team functioning. That is a very different kind of unwillingness to work in the team compared with someone who finds the team exercises difficult or even embarrassing.

It is also necessary to distinguish the nature of the job from the personality. So, for instance, the policy officer should clearly understand that without full engagement with the team the job is probably impossible to carry out effectively. Any sense of withdrawal from the team for a person in that post would need to be handled very differently from, say, the person in the post of office junior. Encouragement and support can be given to the latter to bring them into the team, in the fullest sense of the word, but there will be a lot less pressure than with the former, where every bit of their work will probably be dependent on the team as a whole.

Limits

However much the director or even some of the staff wish to see everyone engaged to the full in building the team, there are limits to what can be asked of people. Staff members should not be pressed or scared by what appears to be required, and which goes beyond the use of their skills to carry out the tasks in their job description. In many small and effective teams it is recognised the staff will frequently give more than is formally required, but the point we are making here is to be aware of the limits and not to push staff beyond them when it is inappropriate to do so.

As an enthusiastic new director, Jim was keen to strengthen the team through a series of team-building exercises, which were duly started. He noticed that one of the secretaries was ill at ease in the exercises. He saw her on her own and said to her: 'You don't seem at all happy with the team exercises, perhaps you would like to tell me why.' Her reply was clear: 'I really don't see that is any of your business.'

Had the limits been reached and, if not, when would they be? Is it unreasonable for a staff member to object to what someone called 'organised play and forced camaraderie'?

Work as an exercise

Exercises to build a team can too easily take place in a vacuum. Even while they are taking place, it is more than likely that some staff will be only too mindful of the work piling up and what needs to be tackled when the exercise or away day is over. They may ask explicitly: 'Shouldn't we be using this time to write the business plan, which we all know is pressing?' That in itself can be a distraction and reduce the effectiveness of their participation. But teams can really come together when they are joined on a task which they all realise has to be completed and is for the benefit of the whole organisation.

Annual reports can be a good example of this. Such reports can be a chore hastily compiled at the last minute by one or two of the staff, published in a hurry with the Chair's name misspelt. More productively, they can be embarked upon almost as soon as the year begins, with all staff being asked to note items which might be included, and with some staff drawn into the process for whom it is a real 'treat' rather than a chore. An outside designer might share her plans for the layout with the team, and so on. It is a staged process with no one excluded and has a product that everyone owns. We have referred earlier in the book to directors who found that the actual process of strategic planning was often more beneficial than the eventual outcome. The real work to be done creates the team spirit.

Going out

Staff will vary as to how much they wish to commit themselves to the team and be involved in everything it does. At the same time, with rare exceptions, people do not wish to be isolated and will want to work in a congenial atmosphere. It is important therefore to have more opportunity to learn something about colleagues and to get to know them beyond their particular role. Team exercises often try to do this. For example, the team may divide into pairs and in each pair the people are asked to tell each other one thing about themselves. This can be interesting but it can be artificial – 'I have six cats'. More valuable and more lasting is for the team from time to time to go out together and for people to learn naturally about each other. Surprising and common interests can be discovered. It is always somewhat sad to learn as a member of staff is leaving that they had a passionate interest in choral music, which just happens to be your interest too. There is a balance between creating opportunities to share things together and wanting to know everyone's business.

Supervision

All staff should have supervision, and in a small team this will generally be provided by the director. For a person who feels that they are not a team person or who has difficulty engaging in the team to the same extent as the others, supervision becomes very important. The process of supervision should help them to enjoy their work and show them how in fact they are acting effectively in the team – people can be surprised to be told that they are in fact a very effective team member. Their diffidence about being a team person will require the director, through supervision, to ensure that the person knows they are taken seriously, that their ideas are heard, that what they think matters and that clear opportunities for development or training will be made available. Important though supervision is, too often in the small organisation it can soon fall into disuse through cancellation and postponement, invariably due to the pressures of the work. A worrying gap between the ideal and the reality opens up.

Conclusion

The issue of an individual not feeling that they are a team person may well not be the biggest problem facing either the team or the director, but it is one which can be seriously misunderstood. Depending on how the views of the team member are expressed, it can be interpreted by the staff as not pulling his or her weight, which is often far from the case. There is a clear need to distinguish an anti-team member of staff from one who does not feel the pull of the team to the same extent as the others and who cannot quite so vigorously salute the team flag.

BEHAVIOUR AT WORK

Introduction

There is much about working in a team that can lie very well hidden from the director. The idiosyncracies, eccentricities and more of individual team members may not always be known to the director, though much may be learned when an individual leaves. We have discussed in an earlier chapter the nature of the familial intensity of a small team with its attendant advantages and disadvantages. For some staff all of the time, and for all staff some of the time, the last thing they want is to leave the pressures of home only to engage with a different set of family pressures an hour or so later. Some feel properly constrained in one setting and much freer in another: for some there can be more licence at work. Sibling rivalries can occur in the team and are no easier to handle than anywhere else; they are certainly no less intense. We need to consider what team members can reasonably expect from each other and where there are limits or boundaries to behaviour at work that might require the director's involvement. But we need also to reflect on what staff's expectations of a director might be. Sauce for the goose is sauce for the gander.

Some common problem areas
The director

Staff expectations of their director will at times be legitimate and at others unreal. There will be enormously different experiences which staff bring with them from other jobs. One female secretary had always done shopping for her previous boss, including choosing his wife's birthday presents, and was relieved to discover the charity director did not require that service. But are there rules of behaviour for the director vis-à-vis the staff? Without wishing to draw up a charter for sainthood, we have heard over the years enough worrying concerns expressed about directors' behaviour. Shouting at staff, serious inconsistency ('we just don't know where we stand'), cancelling supervision, holding on to information, bullying, never just finding the time to talk over things, delegating but checking up every minute and so on.

Directors can and do worry staff, who must have the means to tackle behaviour that troubles them without feeling that the first and only way to do it is through formal grievance procedures. 'I want to have a sense of security at work' was how one staff member put it. People's sense of security is very personal, and this needs to be recognised. At the very least, staff want to be free to comment, not to be always accused of being defensive when defending themselves, and ultimately to be able to 'live' with the director whom they are confident has a 'grip' on the organisation.

My way

The workplace can be the setting for an individual's outbursts or what elsewhere would be called a temper tantrum. Team tolerance of these can be remarkably high, but even so it is often stretched to its limit by the individual who follows up an explosive outburst by saying, 'You don't want to pay any attention to that, it's just my way. It doesn't mean anything.' Senior staff may feel they can get away with such outbursts, which could not be tolerated in junior staff, who then feel unduly constrained.

> Clare, a new administrator, was told on arriving, 'Ignore Richard in the morning as he is always in a bad mood'. But she had to work closely with Richard first thing in the morning as they discussed his incoming mail. She was a woman of some experience and decided to tackle Richard about his moods. She touched a raw nerve and was told, 'you sound just like my mother'.

I do my work

When people are asked questions about discourteous behaviour, they do not as a rule break down and confess; they are just as likely to say, 'No one's ever complained about my work'. There may on occasion be a grudging acceptance along the lines of, 'We all have our faults, no one's perfect'. Asking someone not to slam the door every time they leave the room is scarcely a request to be perfect. But some team members for whatever reason can take a highly functionalist view of team work, namely that as long as everyone does their job well there is no need to be concerned about anything else. Visitors may well be told, 'We all work as a team here', as if there was no contradiction between that and the team's efforts to tolerate and work with difficult behaviour.

Problems at home

Staff are usually very understanding and sympathetic to those team members who are having serious problems at home: sick children, divorce, debt and numerous others. A lot of support can be offered and usually is. This may be the one occasion when personal business properly becomes public concern – though much may depend on how well liked the person was before the crisis arose. On the other hand, staff do expect people to make efforts to tackle their problem and not to wallow in it. 'I really don't want to hear another word about Ann's divorce.' Staff can soon move from sympathy to, 'We've all got problems of one sort or another'. People's capacity to cope with stress at home while at work varies enormously, as does their willingness to share all or part of it. But it is a feature of team life that surfaces more often than people realise, and adds to the demands of the workplace for a very small team.

Not fair

People working closely together develop an acute sense of what is or is not fair. Notions that one or more staff have been treated unfairly can be astonishingly corrosive of team spirit, or that one member of staff has been or is consistently favoured by the director. The office gossip becomes positively inflamed. There can be real issues of discrimination or sexual harassment which must be tackled through the grievance procedures, but what we are touching on here is more the grumbling sense of unfairness, falling well short of serious managerial misdemeanour. It may often be indicative of a wider misunderstanding. A manager expresses concern that the secretary is coming in late, and this is seen as unfair because they 'know' that the youth workers come in 'when they like'. The fact is the secretary needs to be there from nine to five, whereas the youth workers work very different hours, often in the evening. All staff should be treated fairly, but they cannot be treated the same.

Time-keeping

It really should be so simple. The employment contracts state the hours of work. The publicity for the organisation shows clearly when the office is open. Meeting times are agreed in advance. Yet conscientious staff are beside themselves as one or two regularly 'drift in' late. A pattern develops whereby staff operate their own unauthorised flexi-time: 'I always make up the time at the end of the day.' But this takes no account of the work as a whole and the obligations there are for the service to be covered during the agreed hours. Even five minutes regularly shaved off the end of a day can cause problems. Challenging the latter behaviour can quickly be made to seem 'mean', but not doing so leaves other staff wondering why they bother, and a gap appears in previously well-understood expectations.

Off sick

Nowhere is the issue of fairness felt more keenly than over the question of sick leave. Teams will make heroic efforts to cover and assist when a team member is seriously ill or has been injured in an accident. Emergencies at home (the child care arrangements have broken down) are understood. What teams are quick to spot is the regular day or two off sick, just as they are only too well aware of the team member who feels 'entitled' to take the maximum sick leave due to them. They maintain an ominous silence or exchange knowing looks when told that Henry's wife has rung in to say that Henry is sick. Their silence speaks volumes. Then questions start to arise about the arrangements for cover when people are off sick, and the director may be approached 'to do something about Henry'. Fairness is now very much being called into play. But 'doing something' about it may not be that easy. The dubiously sick team member when challenged can too easily respond with, 'Aren't I allowed to be off sick?' The efforts they have made to struggle in, even though not yet fully fit, will be elaborated upon. Having capability policies in place will help deal with this kind of situation, and in any event all organisations should have access to proper legal advice when dealing with such personnel issues.

Arguments by e-mail

Organisations welcome new technology and may make funding applications to secure the means of obtaining the technology. It improves efficiency, enhances job satisfaction and can lend an air of professionalism to the smallest of organisations. Yet it can be used in unexpected ways that need consideration. The administrator and the information officer work 20 feet from each other. The former e-mails the latter about the amount of quality photocopying paper the latter is using. This is met by a resentful e-mail response to the effect that it is not the job of the administrator to question the information officer's photocopying practices. The responses go back and forth. An argument is being held by two staff who work within sight of each other. The e-mails increase in resentment and bad feeling. This happens. The tyranny of the memo is bad enough, but now there are accusatory e-mails appearing on your personal screen. A team's work may become less effective if the e-mail is used to convey strong arguments and hide bruised egos. It may be safer to communicate in this way, it might even be that for less forceful staff the e-mail provides an opportunity denied to them in the more robust personal encounters of the weekly staff meeting, but it can generate inordinate resentment and is an inappropriate use of the new technology.

Confidentiality and confidences

Organisations with a client base will normally have clear rules about confidentiality, how the records are to be kept and to whom they are to be divulged, if at all. But in the hustle and bustle of the workplace other forms of confidentiality arise, particularly in the working relationship between two people, quite often between the director and their secretary, but between others as well. This is a relationship built on trust, perhaps more so than any other.

For some directors their secretaries almost become surrogate partners. Personal confidences can be shared with secretaries, and it comes as a surprise when a seemingly sympathetic secretary promptly gossips about the confidence. Matters relating to the real business in hand might never be divulged, but that the personal confidence finds its way into the office folklore can be hurtful and surprising, and it is by no means easy to deal with.

Responses
Shared ethos

Much of the troublesome behaviour that goes on within the staff team has to be managed and handled by other staff, initially at least. As stated above, the director does not always see it and is not readily told about it. Junior staff in particular have somehow to cope with irascible and difficult senior staff. If it is their first job they may well think this is the norm. This is not healthy, and ultimately either the team or the team with the director have to find ways of managing untoward behaviour. There is therefore an urgent need for a shared ethos, which establishes the workplace as neither a therapeutic community nor a machine shop. The value of the work and of the organisation lies in between, and the team, with the director's help, need to establish the ground rules about managing behaviour. It would be to misunderstand the ethos for anyone to lapse into childish behaviour.

Supervision not therapy

As is so often the case, the essential routine of considered and careful supervision is important, and it is through this mechanism that the discussion of an individual's behaviour in the team and its effect upon a team can be initiated. But it is vital to recognise that supervision is not therapy and it is not its aim to change people's personalities. There is a world of difference between tackling people who may have broken confidences or been consistently rude to a junior member of staff, and trying to get someone to be more forthcoming in the staff meeting. There is a point at which the director has to cut the losses and accept the essential personality of every individual. But for the member of staff, that is not a licence to behave as they wish because 'it is just the way I am'.

Boundaries

Efforts have been made by all to maintain the boundaries between home and work, between who you are and your role in the job, between harmless office gossip and hurtful personal disclosures. The boundaries are not visible and may need to be learned over time, but they are real. If there is serious confusion about the boundary, then what results is the pathology of discordant team behaviour. When all the problems from outside come into the office the work suffers. It is not possible to act just as you want, and in the workplace there has to be self-discipline. In one sense it is important that people act parts in order to get the work done. Senior staff in particular have to be careful not to take offence easily: bridling at others' criticism may produce an excessive reaction damaging to more junior staff. There is a need to 'act' responsibly: the boundary between self and role has to be carefully patrolled.

Change

At times of significant change, especially the appointment of a new director, it is likely that the team will exhibit much more difficult behaviour than normally. The insecurity is inevitable, and there is a real coming together of the personal and the political. Unusual team behaviour may occur during the change itself, or it may surface later when it becomes apparent that the new director is so very different from the old. A team may have been 'kept under' by a director who was a veritable martinet. They now find they have a new director open to ideas, willing to listen and operating a much more liberal regime. This has many benefits, but one of the side effects may well be staff behaviour that is a reaction to what has gone before – the lid has been lifted off the pressure cooker. This can result in turbulent times, in the short term at least, with some staff quite surprised at their own behaviour. Here time will be of the essence in managing the behaviour.

Conclusion

The world is full of many and varied personalities, and most of these will be going to work. It is not surprising therefore that organisations will have within them a range of people and personalities, resulting from time to time in manifestations of curious, difficult or outrageous behaviour. We have only been able to illustrate a handful of examples, but behaviour at work never ceases to surprise: the regular theft of all the office biscuits; the frequent urgent phone calls to the hairdresser; the missing yoghurts; the unposted mail in a drawer.

In thinking about any of this behaviour it is important to ask three questions.

- Why does this behaviour occur?
- Who should do what about it?
- How much does it matter?

Wrestling with the answers to these questions should point the way forward to what is the most appropriate response.

DEPARTMENTS

Introduction

From time to time in this book we have used musical or orchestral analogies, but nowhere is this more appropriate than in thinking about departments and their relationships with each other. For example, in an orchestra the brass section when playing full out is not able to hear the string section. Each section of the orchestra is therefore dependent on the conductor to ensure there is harmony between them and that the ultimate output makes musical sense. In a string quartet each has to rely on the others and teamwork is of the essence. Ironically, as some of the revelations about the behind-the-scenes problems of the Amadeus String Quartet showed, it is possible for a string quartet to produce beautiful music yet for there to be bitter personality feuds between the players. That is perhaps the musical equivalent of the football studies showing how some unpopular players were passed the ball significantly less than others. In short, whether departments are just a single individual as in a small organisation or considerable enterprises in their own right as in a large organisation, they are likely to have views of each other that affect the work of the whole organisation. It is interesting to hear the comments of Labour ministers who found that it was much easier to work together when in opposition than when responsible for departments with their own ethos, requirements and territory. Departments are in their turn small teams, and for the heads of them there will be all the challenges that we have discussed in detail in the chapter on the director.

Points of stress
Administration

At some time most departments feel they are shouldering an undue burden, that they are carrying the organisation and are insufficiently appreciated. This can be particularly common with the administration, often a single-person department in a small organisation or one or two people in a larger one. Administrators generally have to work regular office hours, whereas others may have more flexible hours and even work at home on occasions; they do not go out to meetings or on to the streets or visit other agencies; they may be called upon to explain to callers where other members of the team are. They can too easily become the depository for a miscellany of tasks that do not obviously or easily fit anywhere else.

Because of all this they need to be especially treasured and certainly not taken for granted. They can be the 'rock' of the organisation. Often, however, they do not receive as much management supervision as the frontline service-providers whose work is so 'stressful'. A receptionist with five years of superb work acted as administrator for three months. Within six weeks she complained about how she was being put upon and taken for granted.

> Anna, the administrator and book-keeper, had been one of the key staff through a number of team changes. She valued the work of the agency but felt undervalued herself. She decided to make her presence known through the office message book with details of who left the office when and what was the time of return, with comments such as, 'Tony went on a visit but was back an hour later than he said he would be'. She was well aware that everyone read the message book. She was soon engaged in a discussion about her role and work.

Confusion over agenda and values

Staff are appointed to the team or the department for a particular skill which may relate to finance, direct services, policy, administration, information, reception, and so on. The skills, and the training that has gone into producing them, generate their own values and produce a close working together in that particular section or department. They may, as a small group, feel that they face particular dangers or difficulties, as might an outreach team on the streets or hostel workers dealing with a demanding client group. Others in the organisation will not understand this experience. The understanding that everyone is working for the same end for the same organisation becomes lost in the strength of the department's own agenda. A very strong belief develops in their own skills to tackle the problems they face – 'no one knows the trouble **we**'ve seen'.

If its own agenda becomes paramount, a department can start taking unilateral decisions which suit them but may have serious repercussions for others.

> Jackie, an experienced finance officer, decides that for the better handling of the complex financial administration and to save money for the charity, the finance department will only pay the bills every other month. Within days the training department is demanding an explanation and indeed a reversal of the unilateral decision. The training tutors, who are freelance, have to be paid promptly, and failure to do so will certainly jeopardise the training programme, by which the charity sets so much store.

Departments can decide to pull up the drawbridge, and then teamwork across the organisation will be well-nigh impossible. '**We** produced all the information in time, and the fact that **they** didn't send it out as required is not our responsibility.' Individuals and departments understandably protect themselves but cannot work in isolation. The charitable goal of the organisation is the goal for all and is their *raison d'être*. Hence, if one department fails to deliver on behalf of the whole organisation, the work of others may be imperilled. Actions have repercussions and the latter cannot easily be limited to one department. It may well be that they are felt far from the department which was allegedly at fault. The funding application for the extra hostel worker fails because the statistics from the information department were inaccurate. It is the hostel which has to battle on without the extra worker.

Incomprehension

Departments quite quickly develop their own language, which is helpful and necessary for its daily work, but can create barriers with others. The social workers are preoccupied with the empowerment of the clients, whereas the finance workers wrestle with the implications of SORP, the new charitable accounting guidelines. Any department at any time is capable of becoming maddening in its own mystique. Even when asked questions about the nature of their work, a secretive style can develop, as if it is not appropriate for others to understand. 'They do not need to know what we do in order to do their work properly. Indeed, perhaps they should spend less time trying to understand what we do and concentrate on their own work. After all, we are not interested in what they do.'

Power

Some departments may well not be as interested in the work of others primarily because they have considerable power. In government, discussion quickly focuses on the Treasury, which has been generous and enabled a department to do well or has been particularly difficult and prevented action from being taken. So it can be in small voluntary organisations. There is probably more power lying with the accounts department than with any other part of the organisation. Its role therefore becomes particularly important, so that all the other departments need to understand its workings and thinking.

Departments, like individuals, do not always realise the power they hold in their respective spheres. Directors and heads of departments may well hold a lot of power, particularly if they keep information to themselves. But so much information may pass through them that it is easy to forget to share it on a regular basis. The problem is that simple forgetfulness can too easily be interpreted as a conspiracy against the rest, because just sometimes it is.

Response

There is a need for all members of the organisation, including the director, to acknowledge the value and importance of departments having a belief in their own special skills and abilities to tackle the problems relevant to those departments. But, beyond that, there needs to be an ethos established, whereby departments, normally through the head, or the individual if they are single-member departments, recognise that they have a duty to explain how they relate to others and how they wish others to relate to them. This is not achieved through flowcharts but through explanations in plain English. This has to operate for all departments. Nothing should be arcane.

It is particularly important that departments understand the points of pressure faced by other departments. Everyone knows that at the time of the audit the finance officers face particular stress, but this is not necessarily explained to others, just accepted by them. Other members of the team may in fact benefit from knowing what the finance department actually has to do and may discover how they can help to ease the pressure. Similarly, hostel staff may need to explain just what is involved when they face an inspection from the local social services department.

Conclusion

Just as the conductor of an orchestra has the ultimate responsibility for ensuring that all sections of the orchestra play together in harmony, so the director of a voluntary organisation has the responsibility to ensure that departments work with each other towards the common goal. But the director cannot will this to happen and depends on the readiness of departments to communicate with each other and to understand that each department is doing everything possible to achieve the organisation's goals. There has to be some trust that members of all departments are developing their particular skills and using them to their utmost within the department. The conductor of the orchestra can do very little if the brass players have simply not been practising.

chapter 4

STAFF AND COMMITTEE

Introduction

Even the smallest voluntary organisation has its distinct component parts, and any gaps in understanding between them can be problematic at best and destructive at worst. An area which is particularly prone to misunderstanding is the relationship between the staff and the committee. We have known warfare to occur between these two, with staff 'invading' the committee. The director cannot always be the bridge between the two, even though he or she knows the staff and the committee well and is often the conduit of information between them. Staff, however, have their own perspective on the committee and its role. If this is allowed to become too negative, the director can be placed in a very difficult position, will have divided loyalties and will need to work 'both sides of the track' to correct the situation.

Concerns and misgivings

What do they know?

Staff, who may be very experienced in their field, can be bemused, puzzled or angry over a committee making a decision without any apparent relevant experience. The more the committee seeks to be 'hands-on', the more the staff will feel this. Staff want to be left to get on with their job, and the more pressurised the job (queues of clients) the more this is likely to be the case. Support and supervision from the manager are valued, but not intrusive decisions by the committee, 'not one of whom has ever worked at the coalface'. Similarly, in the statutory sector there have been recent expressions of concern about lay school governors, some of whom through their unannounced visits are seen as 'meddlesome'.

A staff belief takes hold that to be on the management committee it is essential to know a great deal about the work. That may not necessarily be right, especially if the committee is clear about the limits of its role, in which case a close working knowledge of the staff's activities may well be unnecessary. Staff might find that a committee composed of people who, say, have all run hostels was a committee that was far too close to the work for comfort. The committee might end up spending all its time second-guessing the workers on the ground:

`We always found it was best to … '. There would in effect be two staff teams, one full-time and one part-time: a recipe for disaster. Committees where most of the members are peers of the director can have not dissimilar results. This is an issue to which too little attention is paid and which for some organisations poses an acute dilemma. But in some parts of the voluntary sector there is a very limited choice of committee members with relevant experience and knowledge, for instance in the refugee world, so that those organisations may have to rely unduly on peer management.

Who are they?

As we have noted in an earlier chapter, committee members may not always know much about each other and they may also know little about the staff. It took one committee member a long time to go round the offices and see that five of the twelve staff were black, so that some concerns about equal opportunities became less pressing. For staff, the committee can be even more of a mystery. Who are they? How were they selected?

> 'I don't care who they are as long as they let me get on with my job.'
> 'I haven't seen the tall man in a dark suit before.' 'No, he doesn't come very often.'
> 'Is the smartly dressed woman a new committee member?' 'No, she's the auditor.'

The permutations are real and endless. The staff's unawareness of the committee may be feigned, and efforts to inform them of the committee membership may well have fallen on stony ground. Staff can develop a culture in which it is *de rigueur* to disparage the committee. It is seen as the director's job to worry about the committee, not the staff's. But there can also be real ignorance on the staff's part which can only heighten anxiety, especially, for example, when grants are not forthcoming and there is talk of having to reduce the working hours.

Attending committees

To help bridge the gap between staff and committee the former can be invited to attend the meeting as a general principle, and will in any event attend if they have to speak to a specific item. This can work well but it can also have some unintended consequences. Staff may outnumber the committee, who can come to feel 'threatened' by the experts in attendance. Staff may want to speak on items but be unsure whether they can and, if they do, what weight their views will carry. Reports, diligently produced by staff, may not have been read by the committee or, worse, may have been read and not properly understood.

A staff group of a social work agency spent many hours working on policy proposals for the committee, at the committee's request. One committee member exploded and said she never again wanted to see the word 'society' in any document produced by the agency. The discussion was shelved.

Such vagaries of committee behaviour, to which reference was made in an earlier chapter, may leave some staff feeling a distinct lack of confidence in the body which has *legal* responsibility for the organisation. 'The present committee is really terrible. I wouldn't want them out there representing us.' Then, having spent several hours late one evening attending the committee, staff may ask for time off in lieu, which horrifies the committee who have given up their time voluntarily. More gaps in understanding appear.

Helping or managing?

All staff, but especially staff new to the committee world, feel particularly upset or aggrieved when their ideas and proposals are amended or seriously criticised or when the committee asks that new work be undertaken. A sense of not being appreciated or of the demands of the work being seriously underestimated soon surfaces. Whether the staff have been at the meeting or not, frustration and incomprehension envelops them. This can be heightened when committee members have, in the eyes of the staff, paid too much attention to petty detail, for example asking that paragraphs be numbered or that recommendations be set out more clearly. 'They were lucky to get the report at all.' An apparently brusque criticism of a report can lead to considerable anger in a staff member – sometimes because the writer knows deep down that the committee was right. Under pressure the staff come to see the committee as 'letting them down'. The committee is surely there to help and support them. Notions of governance disappear.

The director

The team sees the director as their advocate at the committee, batting for them. Concerned to secure funds for a much needed new post, they may not appreciate the committee's decision to defer consideration of that and give priority instead to their own concern about health and safety matters. How has this happened? Did the director really back the proposal? The team may feel that the director has allowed the Chair to push through a 'wheeze' and may comment that, 'We all know the Chair has another agenda'. The team may be sorry that the director had a very bruising four-hour committee meeting, but that is part of the job. For the team, their expectations and the high hopes of the meeting have not been realised, and that is what matters. The director has loyalties and confidences in two directions, which the team may not readily acknowledge. They do not want to hear from the director that 'You have no idea how difficult the job is'. For some directors the monthly or quarterly committee meeting can be intensely stressful, as the gap between team and committee becomes ever more apparent. And on the morning after the meeting an unexpected problem may surface.

The morning after

The senior staff member and the director have both attended a long and difficult committee meeting. The next morning the staff member, who is not tied to the committee in the same way as the director, feels free to, and more importantly needs to, explode about the seeming incompetence of the committee. Variations on 'they're impossible' or 'they have no idea' fill the air. Staff, loyal to their colleague, commiserate, and the legitimate authority of the committee is undermined in practice, though not legally. The director, whose agenda for action from the committee is already long enough, now has to present to the team the committee's position and the realities of how they have to work within the committee's decisions. This is made much more difficult by the pre-emptive strike delivered by the colleague.

Responses
Informing staff

All staff need to be clearly informed both about the role of the committee and who the members of it are. For staff who are new to working in the voluntary sector, the role of the committee can be quite confusing, and the situation should not be allowed to develop where ambiguity develops around the respective roles of the committee and the director. Failing to understand the function of the committee can leave uninformed staff wondering about the exact authority of the director.

It is just as important that the staff are informed about the members of the committee. This is naturally much easier in smaller organisations. It is helpful for staff to have photographs and potted biographies of the committee members. No assumption should be made that staff know about them just because the director is so familiar with them. The fact that one of the committee is a famous public figure who writes regularly in the *Guardian* does not necessarily mean that they are known to all. When there is a new Chair, or indeed any new officer is appointed to the committee, it is valuable for the new appointee briefly to meet all the staff, where the size of the organisation makes this practical.

Guidelines for committee attendance

It is important that the director and the Chair reach a clear agreement about staff attendance at committee meetings. Directors can put everyone in a difficult position if, just as the meeting is about to begin, the Chair is informed by the director that, 'I've asked staff to attend because they are concerned about the way the organisation is going.' It is virtually impossible at that stage for the Chair to say no to their attendance, and the agenda of the committee has in a subtle way been rewritten. Committee members suddenly appearing at a staff meeting would raise anxiety, and so does the reverse.

Rules for attendance by staff at committee meetings can be clearly laid down and understood by both parties. Staff can be present, for example, to speak to their own papers. There could well be a rota for a member of staff to observe committee procedures. There could be occasions when it is important for all staff to attend with the agreement of the Chair if there is a matter to be discussed that will affect all members of staff. But even then the rules of engagement need to be clear, so that the committee do not feel driven to make a particular decision because of the staff presence which itself subtly undermines or subverts their trustee role.

Reporting back

Any reporting back needs to be linked to a prior discussion at the staff meeting when they have had briefly explained to them what is on the committee agenda and why. It is essential to take every step possible to try and reduce the mystery of the process.

There needs to be a structure for the director to report back to the staff from the committee meeting. This should be a report *from* the committee, not *on* the committee. This would include the summary of the decisions made and the reasons for them and the outline of any difficulties that the committee faced in reaching a particular decision. All decisions that were taken should be included in the report, even though at first glance they might not seem relevant to the whole staff group. It is surprising how staff may make links with the information they receive which can draw them in more closely to the organisation.

Committee members at staff meetings

From time to time committees have to consider very difficult items directly affecting staff: pay, general conditions of service, new pension arrangements, an office move, and so on. It is not helpful on these occasions to leave all the reporting back to the director, who, after all, is equally affected by these matters. Much can be gained by having the relevant committee member, not necessarily always the Chair, attend a staff meeting and explain the thinking of the committee around the particular proposal or decision. If this can be done during the decision-making process rather than simply after the deed has been done, then so much the better. Familiarity again becomes important.

Conclusion

Manifestly, staff and committee have different roles and functions, but it should not be a case of 'never the twain shall meet'. Neither should the informality, rightly much prized in small voluntary organisations, become so dominant that the work of the committee is impeded. The committee need to be sensitive to the implications of their decisions, and should be informed by the director accordingly. Measures need to be taken on the other hand to ensure that all staff fully understand the work of a committee in a voluntary organisation and its particular, even peculiar, role.

SECTION 4
Outsiders

'They poke their stick into the ant hill and then go away.'

'Monitoring just drives us to go for the low-hanging fruit.'

'We genuinely want to help the organisation but they
are so resistant.'

The outsider's tale

'We try to make it very clear that we are there to help and not
to pass judgement or deliberately find fault. They do, of course,
have to understand that we are bound by our own rules and
regulations, which determine much of what we have to do.
Turning a blind eye to anything is in no one's interest. It can be
tense when we visit initially, but we stress to our staff the need
to take account of the pressures the organisation is under. One
of the curious things for us is that it varies enormously as to
whom we deal with. We don't often see the Chair and on
occasion we even have to make a point of asking to see the
director. Maybe our visit inadvertently finds some gaps in the
organisation, which somehow we are then blamed for. Let us be
honest, sometimes the ant hill needs to be stirred up.'

Introduction

A key feature in the life of voluntary organisations is the amount of engagement there has to be with outsiders, some of whom could certainly be described as 'OFVOL'. The director will often be the key figure in handling events in this border territory, but it is by no means exclusively their role. The treasurer and finance officer will be closely involved in audit matters. The Chair will need to meet with any regulatory body. Staff may need to meet with funders. It is a highly varied and variable picture. But just who are the outsiders who from time to time come into the life and work of a voluntary organisation? They include:

- funders
- auditors
- Charity Commission
- lawyers
- regulators such as the Housing Corporation (which is also a major funder)
- inspectors such as the local authority
- investment managers.

Only the larger organisations are likely to be affected by all of these, but small organisations will certainly have relationships with auditors and funders. Rather than discuss the relationship with each outsider in turn, we have tried to look at some of the general issues that arise, paying particular attention, implicitly at least, to funders and auditors.

We would also acknowledge that government can often be a major outside influence, but it is involved much less personally with the organisations and therefore we have not attempted to consider its impact in any detail. All organisations are affected by employment legislation such as the 1999 Employment Relations Act, which has a multitude of small but vital changes touching every organisation. Other legislation, such as Asylum and Immigration Acts, can really shape the work and direction of the relevant bodies, even on occasion against their better judgement.

Issues that arise
Scrutiny

It is generally accepted that part of good governance is that scrutiny should be exercised naturally throughout and within an organisation. But it becomes a distinctly different matter when the scrutiny comes from outside. A degree of anxiety is generated about an independent assessment, whatever its purpose. The analogy of the examination is never far from people's minds, especially as the exam is unseen. There are many questions in the air.

- What will the judgement be?
- Will it be well informed and impartial?
- If there is an adverse report on the organisation, what will the consequences be for the organisation and the work?
- Will we be found to be somehow 'in the wrong'?

A great deal of time will be spent on preparing funding applications, and funders will be asked, 'Have we got it right?' If the application fails, the director often wants to know 'where we got it wrong'. There is so often that worrying assumption that it had to be 'wrong', rather than acceptance of the fact that there were just too many applications. For a time at least the outsider, and the funder above all, appears to have considerable power, and it is not always clear just how the exercise of that power can be challenged, should there be a need to do so.

Frustration

Statutory funders have produced what one charity calls a 'plethora of monitoring'. This organisation feels that inefficiency has been elevated to an art form. 'We were audited 12 times a year on a grant of £100,000.' Too often accountability is equated with counting ability, and the purpose of improving service delivery is lost sight of. One agency submitted detailed statements of outcomes to its government funder only to find a year later that these were never read. The completion of the forms had become the test of effectiveness.

Uncertainty

Although auditors and inspectors may visit every year, and although there may be quite frequent funding applications being made, there can still be considerable uncertainty around the processes. This may be particularly the case where an auditor is only involved with one or two charities and therefore has relatively little experience of the world of the voluntary sector. It needs to be clear just what is being inspected, audited or guaranteed.

But uncertainty can also arise around the concepts used by both parties. Major funders, for example, including government, make funds available for the purposes of the rehabilitation and the resettlement of particular client groups. With that money they expect voluntary organisations to rehabilitate and resettle vulnerable people. But it can transpire that the service-providers develop a very different understanding of what is meant by such terms compared with the funders. Funders of schemes to 'resettle' homeless people have been said by some to be 'naïve and unrealistic' about the speed of 'throughput', as very long periods of assessment may well be needed before referral on can take place. As one field worker put it, 'Resettlement is about offering people choices not forcibly dispersing them'. The funders' ideas will not be informed by the practice on the ground, whereas they believe that the practitioners' views are too driven by the day-to-day work, which almost inevitably makes the concepts more and more uncertain as time goes on. In the beginning the desire to get something done often makes the niceties of definition seem unnecessary and too time-consuming, but they are bound to rear their head at some point and usually in debate with an outsider.

Values

Some of the uncertainty can also arise from the fact that the outsider will often have a very different value base from that of the voluntary organisation. This may be particularly marked in the case of auditors, statutory funders or regulatory bodies. They are there to help the voluntary organisation but from a quite different standpoint and with their own system of accountability. It may well not be appropriate for them to become over-concerned with just how difficult the work of the organisation really is. However, the different starting points of the two organisations, the outsider and the insider, can lead to serious disenchantment, particularly among the staff.

'These people seem incapable of understanding what we do here.'
'Their values are very narrow and completely at variance with ours.'
'They just seem to want "tangible" results.'

There is a frequent theme which emerges, namely that the outsider has a narrow value base, whereas the insider's is so much more all-embracing, even visionary. Monitoring forms and reports in particular bring about an apparent clash of values. Too often voluntary organisations feel that they are being asked to compress their work into boxes with ticks, or just give yes or no answers to questions, with far too little opportunity to explain the complexities of the work they are doing. Accompanying letters are often sent with the forms, putting a gloss on the figures provided and hoping that all will be sympathetically received. Even then there is no sure way of knowing whether the qualifications and caveats that are being entered will somehow mean that the organisation is marked down or whether their honesty and endeavour will be appreciated. For the organisation which is doing the monitoring, there is a thin line between explaining and explaining away.

Expectations

In the engagement with the outsider there can be a 'seething mass of expectations', not all of which are openly expressed or committed to paper. It is important to try and be aware of some of these. The more obvious expectations will be agreed beforehand, so that, for example, the auditors as part of their visit will set down just what they need to have in the way of prepared documentation, working space and access to files. The formally declared expectation should not present any problem, but it is the undeclared expectation which may generate the anxiety.

The committee, who may feel somewhat distant from auditors, funders or inspectors, may hope that they will not get any nasty surprises. They will believe that if they have done their job well during the year this will be the case.

The staff will expect that the director, or their line managers, will ensure that their work is presented in the best possible light, so that they will be able to get on with their job, properly and securely funded. They will not want their personal or professional security in any way to be put at risk, and that will be the minimum expectation.

The director will feel they have most to gain and most to lose from any outsider's verdict: praise and self-esteem if all goes well; blame if all goes badly. In fact, if not in law, the buck does stop with the director, as it is the director who has been overseeing and managing the work of the organisation. Directors will feel themselves to be the main players, with the others to a greater or lesser extent witnesses, as the outsiders descend upon the organisation.

The outsiders too have their expectations. As voluntary organisations are so dependent on funders, the expectations of the latter become paramount. Confused communications with a funder can be extremely detrimental to the organisation and hence every effort needs to be made to clarify just what the funders' expectations are. Much attention will be given to ensure that all the papers and arguments are produced in order to support the funding application. But, when it is successful, there may be less clarity about what is then expected, and this may be true for both sides.

- How much reporting back will be needed and how often?
- What form will any monitoring take?
- Does the funder want reports specifically produced for them or will the normal committee reports suffice?
- If there are several funders, as there often are, is the organisation expected to produce different reports for each funder?
- How honest can an organisation be about the difficulties it is encountering, which could certainly not have been anticipated at the time of the funding application?

All this and more needs to be clarified. Funding relationships are as important as the funds themselves.

Who is in control?

The handling of the relationship with the outsider will invariably raise questions about the nature of the control and management within the organisation. A great deal of information will flow between the organisation and the auditor or funder, and for the auditor the culmination of their work is a formal report. Much of all this will be handled by the director, and it may depend on how the relationship between the director and the Chair or committee is operating just how much information gets passed through to them. The content of the auditor's concerns may not be openly and fully communicated. Although much may be clear about the day-to-day interaction between director, Chair and committee, when an outsider enters the scene there may be need for a change in practice, so there should be discussion beforehand within the organisation as to how the outsider's material will be handled.

When the organisation takes the initiative to approach a funder the question of control also arises. Directors and senior staff tend to drive the funding applications and meet with the funders. Chairs and committee members are not often involved, except with very large funding applications to statutory bodies or the Lottery. Keen to secure funding and feeling sure that this is what the committee would want, directors may find that they have gone a long way down the road, even the whole way, with a funding application before the committee is aware of what is happening. Funders may begin to see what some of the issues of control are within the organisation as they process the application. But they will need to be clear about how much they can appear to be 'intervening' in the overall management of the organisation on the back of a particular funding application. A director may not expect that the funder will or should be so concerned about internal management issues, not least because the work they are doing is manifestly needed and, above all, is seen as successful.

Ways forward
Acknowledging the value

While any outside intervention in an organisation can be difficult, this does not have to be the norm, and one way of preparing the ground is to acknowledge within the organisation the value of outside scrutiny. The money which has been given to the organisation will be for the donor a form of investment – they have chosen your organisation to fund rather than another because they wish to see things done in areas of concern to them. It is reasonable therefore that you reassure them that the money has been used well; winners, after all, will attract more investment.

One way of persuading staff that, say, the gathering and production of monitoring and evaluation data is something more than one chore too many would be to ask: if the funders had not asked us to do this, should we not be deciding to do it for ourselves in any event? Having good internal systems looking at what the organisation does and does not do, and how it intends to bridge that gap, will go halfway to meeting the inevitable encounter with the outsider.

At its best an outsider's scrutiny can bring to assessing the quality of the work an objectivity that is not achieved easily, if at all, from inside. It is not open to suspicion of partisanship or axe-grinding. This presumes that the scrutiny is not ignorant or pettifogging. But in one particular regard the outsider's scrutiny can bring the ultimate guarantee of quality: it can draw on useful comparisons and bring an external dimension and breadth of vision that is less easily found from within.

Sharing information

Although, at any one time, perhaps only one or two staff or committee members may be directly involved in a particular negotiation or engagement with the outsider, it is important to keep everyone else informed. Uncertainty breeds anxiety, which is reduced if the purpose of a visit is explained – whether it is the auditors or the Lottery assessor who is expected. If it is a formal inspection of a residential hostel, everyone can be clear about what may or may not be asked or what is likely to take place. If questions are asked in advance this will reduce any unnecessary element of surprise.

Sharing language

Outsiders who are concerned with an organisation's performance may use language which needs to be clarified before any firm engagement occurs. It is far too late to do this after the reports have been written and sent to the funder. We have read reports which use almost interchangeably terms like 'aims', 'targets', 'objectives', 'outputs', 'results', 'outcomes', 'ultimate goal'. Outsiders and insiders need to agree what this language is saying.

Sharing purpose

If the relationship between the outside agency and the charity is to be as fruitful as possible, there needs to be some congruence of purpose. Some organisations feel that they provide statistics for the outside body which pay no attention to the quality of the work. Worse interpretations are then put upon the figures which take no account of the work. No service-provider is happy with poor performance, and they want to work with relevant outsiders to ensure the best performance possible. Both sides should be in the business of meeting needs, albeit from different vantage points, so that developing and sharing a common purpose becomes self-evidently good sense.

Relationships

Wherever possible, visits from the outsiders should not be confined to one-off events, but rather efforts should be made to establish a relationship with the bodies involved which may prove of value over time and certainly on the occasion of the next inspection. Auditors have financial management experience, which might be called upon during the year, especially if there are any unexpected problems within the finance department. The committee may take comfort from knowing that the auditors are on hand should the need arise and that there is a friendly ear if they have any untoward anxieties.

Funders and funded can continue to learn from each other, not least about what it is reasonable to expect and to provide once a grant has been given. Organisations may even ask funders to talk together about their monitoring demands, which seem to be endless and are so time-consuming. Learning from mistakes as well as successes can benefit both parties, but this is best achieved within a continuing relationship.

Their job

It has to be openly and clearly recognised that the outsider is performing a different function from that of the organisation, and that rules and regulations govern them just as much as they do the organisation itself. Accountancy regulations become ever more intricate, and these are not something that auditors can lightly ignore. Through their expertise and an objective scrutiny auditors do in fact discover things, just as funders through their particular approach may cause the organisation to think again about certain courses of action. This is all legitimate and, if it takes place within the context of the relationship referred to above, can be of inestimable benefit to the organisation. Even though it is their job, an outsider should guard against introducing too many 'oughts' into any report without some clear understanding as to how they might be realised. That 'there ought to be higher staffing levels' might well be known to the organisation, and all that stops the implementation is much-needed funding.

Conclusion

Borders are notorious for being areas of friction, tension and even warfare. Managing that border area is no easier in organisations than it is in countries. Bringing to it as much definition as possible therefore becomes paramount. There is also a need for reassurance, so that the director will have to be clear with staff and committee just what is happening and who is required to do what. It may only be to say that 'everything is under control'. But the inherent tension in some of the relationships with outsiders should not be underestimated. Committees can become incandescent with rage when the report from the outside body is addressed to a Chair long since retired or sent to the old address.

CONCLUSIONS

There are now nearly 200,000 registered charities, with as many voluntary organisations again that are not eligible to register or have chosen not to do so. Not all these organisations are in difficulties at any one time. Some may be fortunate and throughout their history avoid any serious difficulties. But many, for a time at least, come up against real problems of the sort which we have discussed in this book, and a smaller number go through extremely troubled times. This companion is a guide to help think about and deal with some of those more difficult times. We have tried to address some of the concerns which managers, committee members and staff talk about, but which do not often feature in the orthodox management texts. Sometimes it is easier for directors to work on major business plans rather than deal with the abrasive notice pinned up in the kitchen: 'Didn't your parents teach you to wash up?' But the good feeling generated by the meeting in relation to the business plan soon evaporates when staff see the kitchen notice.

On occasions we have thought that we might be exaggerating a particular difficulty. But when we discussed any specific issue with Chairs, directors or staff, it soon emerged that it was scarcely possible to over-emphasise the intensity of the problems that can arise in a small organisation, and no doubt larger ones too. Chairs have said that at each meeting the director never appears to have done anything agreed at the previous meeting, and wonder what the director is actually doing. Staff have talked of a director standing on the table and shouting at them in staff meetings. Directors have regaled us with accounts of crises over milk in the fridge or the supply of biscuits as well as much weightier matters. Organisations and, more important, the people within them can become seriously side-tracked by issues that seem for a time to overwhelm and take over part of the organisation. We ourselves have been embroiled in many such situations, and hence this book is written with real affection, for we are concerned to try and provide some guidance for those working at all levels in small voluntary organisations. Sometimes there are not answers to be had but rather clues and hints at the way forward.

As we wrote, various themes emerged for us that we wish to highlight in this concluding section.

Complexity

It is important to recognise and acknowledge that, just because the organisation is small – three staff, a few volunteers and five people on the committee – this does not mean that management is simple. The complexities are all there, and it is not necessarily the fault of the director or the committee that conflicts surface and prevent the organisation from operating as it should. They are inherent in the nature of the creature, but it is not inevitable that people should be overwhelmed by them. Apparently small steps forward can bring far greater organisational complexity than appears at first sight. A wise Chair once said that as soon as the first resident is admitted to the hostel the organisation is changed. Similarly, the Chairs and committees of small organisations can be quite surprised at what is required of them when the first paid member of staff is appointed.

Team

We all value working in a team, know that a good team is more than the sum of its parts, and also know just how terrible it is to be in a workplace with no team spirit. Yet all of us, and managers in particular, should guard against using the concept as a spray-on word without being aware of all the hard work that has to go into making the concept real. It will mean different things to different people. Team expectations will vary. Working in a team has to bring out the best not only in you but also in the team. Exhortations by directors to staff to be good team performers might reasonably be met with 'Can you be more specific?' They can equally evoke an anxiety about expectations which some staff may believe they cannot meet.

Routes

Organisations do not, as it were, spring forth fully formed. Their committee members and staff all arrive via different routes, which need to be understood and taken into account. The director may have had a real longing to obtain the job, seeing it as offering potential to work with a particular group in need as well as personal fulfilment. But the Chair may be much less enthusiastic, even feeling that he or she has been press-ganged into the role. There are dozens of variations on this theme; it is an inescapable part of the fabric of the organisation.

History and culture

It is important not to be too cavalier about the history of the organisation. We can overdo distancing ourselves from the past. How an organisation has arrived at the position it now occupies needs understanding and remembering. The committee will normally have been in place before the staff, and could have a different understanding of the culture from that of the staff team. The culture of the organisation will greatly influence how change is handled. It may not be easy to describe, but one has only to suggest 'merging' with another apparently like-minded organisation to see how quickly strong statements about 'our culture' surface. The past should not act as a prison for the present or the future, but a good understanding of it can often illuminate current conflicts and misunderstanding. That certain departments were in existence before others can become important to remember in resolving inter-departmental disputes. Where organisations have regional offices, the way in which the latter became established can be surprisingly important in matters of management. New directors may well be reminded by committee members of 30 years' standing of what went on all those years ago. It will still be very fresh in some minds!

Values

Voluntary organisations can overdo their emphasis on values, often contrasting themselves favourably with the commercial sector. There is nonetheless a value base to almost all voluntary bodies, and it can be rather taken for granted that everyone shares it simply by virtue of being part of the organisation. This is not necessarily the case, and conflicts can arise unexpectedly when different values surface. Such differences may be between committee members or departments or individuals. Considerable work may need to be done to build bridges between these, though trying to ensure some congruence in the value base before people join the organisation is a less painful process.

Routines

When an organisation is very small, it is tempting to proceed as if informality can be the watchword. The Chair and director meet as and when required, with no apparent need to systematise it. Establishing routines and procedures appears bureaucratic and against the very spirit of the voluntary organisation, but not everyone is equally comfortable without them. Small organisations can suddenly grow with the award of a large Lottery grant, and then it becomes imperative to establish systems. This results in the organisation having to cope not only with the impact of a large grant but with considerable organisational changes as well. Having agreed and clear routines within the management of the organisation is not of itself bureaucratic, nor does it mean that flexibility, risk and innovation have been thrown out of the window. Both approaches are, in our view, essential ingredients of a healthy body.

Courtesy

Good working relationships are usually sustained by the small considerations of life. Difficulties and disagreements in the team over service priorities may be argued out in the appropriate meetings and do not usually lead to angry mutterings. The same cannot be said when Ken has again left the photocopier jammed or Gill failed to notify anyone that she has used the last batch of A4 envelopes. Such discourtesies may be remembered long after the budget debate has been forgotten. Developing and maintaining an ethos of real consideration for each other is not an add-on to management, but a key part of it.

Familiarity

Not everyone can know everything about everyone else's business, even in a quite small organisation. But it becomes dangerous if there are parts of the organisation which are totally unfamiliar with others. There needs to be a conscious policy and effort by everyone to ensure that they are sufficiently acquainted with all the areas of the organisation's work. This applies to both staff and committee members. As we have seen earlier, familiarity breeds respect. Without that basic understanding it is too easy to make rash judgements about the work of others or, much more important, their effectiveness. Committee members, when given even a brief glimpse of the work of some of the staff, may say, 'I had no idea what was involved.' Previously they might well have asked, 'Why aren't more cases being dealt with by the advice workers?'

Awareness

Allied to familiarity is the need to develop an ethos of awareness. People should be aware of the particular pressures on a department, or the impact on the organisation of new government proposals, or the proposed changes in the committee structure, and a host of other items. There should be as little mystery as possible. It is not simply a question of passing out information – the eternal memo – but rather of ensuring that everyone has a chance to understand its implications. Too often difficulties can arise because it is assumed that the mere receipt of the information is sufficient to make people aware. Not everyone is confident enough to say they do not understand, but when people do, they need to be given full attention. The corollary of encouraging awareness of the issues affecting the organisation and familiarity with colleagues' work is to ensure that when people speak they are listened to. Individuals vary enormously in articulacy, and the diffident question is as important to hear as the passionately advanced argument.

Familial model

Workplaces have their own distinct style and tone. For small teams the ethos is critical, and often that ethos draws on the familial model for strength and even inspiration. Home may well be the only other type of 'organisation' to refer to. This, however, can have its drawbacks – not least because familial intensity may be the last thing that the workplace needs. 'I am old enough to be your mother' is not an easy response to handle when a dispute occurs. Professionalism therefore has to have pride of place for the work to be done.

Trust

There has to be a huge amount of trust between the Chair and the director, but it does not stop there. The wealth of close working relationships in even a small organisation is such that trust is an essential glue. A lot goes on that is only seen by a few, and some work is out of sight entirely. Staff have to trust how they are represented by the director at the committee; the director trusts the staff to be doing their jobs in or out of the office; the committee trusts the director to carry out their decisions. Sustaining the climate of trust is vitally important, for if it starts to be eroded it will seriously affect the whole team. Any early signs need to be heeded and action taken; it is too easy to ascribe the warning sign to a personality clash.

Limits

It is important to recognise that, however committed the staff, however pressing the needs and however tenacious the committee members, there is a limit to what can be required of those within the organisation. The committee members are only expected to give their full-time attention on a part-time basis. For staff there is life beyond the organisation: when all is said and done it is only a workplace. Founders of charities, as we have seen, may well create – consciously or otherwise – expectations that few others will be able to match. Developing a sense of what can reasonably be required is an important part of management, although this may not be formally documented.

Power and authority

It is clear that within any organisation some people carry more power or authority than others, which is normally recognised through the positions they hold. The Chair and the director are the two most obvious examples. There will also be those in the organisation who, because of who they are, have considerable authority though little formal power. A problem will arise where the reverse situation exists: someone who ostensibly has considerable power actually carries insufficient authority to use it effectively. Efforts need to be made to ensure that there is the right balance of power and authority – who is really running the organisation? Just as important is that all power is exercised with humanity. Whatever vogue 'naming and shaming' may have in government inspections, it has no place in small voluntary organisations.

Soul

However the organisational charts are written, and whatever the power and authority explicit in the various job descriptions, leaders of organisations need to have what can best be termed 'soul'. Developing trust, listening to others, having a management style in which affection plays a genuine part, all this and more is part of the way to achieve what everyone in the whole organisation wants. And treating people well has to be sustained in the hard times as well as the good.

Change

Change in an organisation produces both excitement and anxiety, and too much of either will impede the process. Changing direction, appointing a new director or Chair, bringing users on to the management committee, all these developments will invariably take much longer than originally planned. A balance is needed between inducing a sense of weariness and making a quick decision that will simply not hold. It is rare for any serious change not to have far more implications for the organisation than appreciated at the outset.

Purpose

The common factor in all the problems we have touched on in this book is that they are all capable of developing a virulent life of their own and actually impeding the work of the organisation. Everyone always tries to assure everyone else that the fundamental work of the organisation has not been affected by the problem, but that is rarely true. At its worst the irresponsibility of self-indulgence takes over, and this can occur in any part of the organisation. Staff can be demoralised by committee behaviour just as easily as the reverse. Management, or indeed staff, have to reinforce people's awareness of what they are there for. The organisation has to meet the needs for which it was established. These cannot be put on hold while internal strife is resolved. The Chair and the director, above all, are charged with ensuring that the organisation does not lose sight of its purpose. Ultimately, that is itself the purpose of this book.

QUESTIONS TO CONSIDER

As we made clear at the outset, this book is not a management manual, and we have therefore not included tasks or exercises within the text. However, we thought it might be helpful to set down some questions that arise from the material. These questions are not a test, but are primarily intended to encourage further thought about the whole business of small organisations. The questions have been grouped under relevant headings.

General

- Where are the gaps in your organisation? How can they best be bridged?

Committee

- Can you think of situations where the Chair, either you or someone you know, has adopted the role of constitutional monarch, benevolent despot or dictator? Was it appropriate and effective? What other roles could the Chair usefully play?
- How did your committee members arrive on the committee? How much do they know about each other?
- When have you or someone you know behaved 'badly' on a committee? What prompted the behaviour, and what was its effect?
- How would you describe the style of your committee? Is it an appropriate style?
- How well organised and presented are the papers for the committee?
- If you have a strategic plan, how often is it referred to?
- When you were last involved in selecting a new director, what were the things that surprised you about the process? How, if at all, would you now do it differently?

Founder

- Are there ways of managing a founder that do not restrict their drive and inspiration but do safeguard the overall management of the organisation?

Director

- What does 'running the organisation' mean to you?
- What is the most isolating thing about your role?

- How much information passes between you and the Chair? Is it too little or too much?
- Is your committee hands-on, hands-off or no hands at all?
- How and when are staff praised or thanked?
- What are you essentially paid to do?

The team

- What does the notion of the team mean to you?
- What systems are in place to help the team function as effectively as possible?
- Are there any practices that work against the team's functioning?
- What are the limits to what you can require of staff in the name of the team?
- Can you think of a team member who is 'anti-team', and one who simply does not feel the pull of the team as strongly as others? Are there any other useful distinctions within a team?
- Think of a particular piece of perplexing or troublesome behaviour at work and ask: Why did it occur? Who should do what about it? How much does it matter?

Departments

- Do all the departments within your organisation share the same values?
- If your organisation is viewed as an orchestra, is one section drowning out another? Can the director hear all sections equally easily?

Staff

- What expectations do you have of the director?
- How well do you know the Chair and the committee?
- How do you handle others' irritating behaviour at work?
- Are there divisions within the team based, for example, on location within the office or who goes out and who stays in?
- How much does the director know about what goes on in the workplace?
- What has been the best team you have worked in and why?

Users

- What are the particular challenges about bringing users on to the management committee? How might the difficulties be overcome?

Outsiders

- Think of a good experience that your organisation has had with an outsider and ask: What made it one? Similarly, consider a bad experience.

FURTHER READING

The books listed below are a valuable source of further information and reflections on management issues in voluntary organisations. Prices were correct in February 2000 but may be subject to change.

Published by the Directory of Social Change (020 7209 5151)

Managing Conflict, Gill Taylor, 1999 (£12.50)

Managing People, Gill Taylor and Christine Thornton, 1995 (£10.95)

Managing Recruitment and Selection, Gill Taylor, 1996 (£11.50)

Developing your Organisation, Alan Lawrie, 2000 (£12.50)

Managing Quality of Service, Alan Lawrie, 1995 (£10.95)

Voluntary Matters: Management and good practice in the voluntary sector, published in association with the Media Trust, 1997 (£16.95)

Books from other publishers, available from the Directory of Social Change (020 7209 5151)

Published by the London Voluntary Service Council

Just about Managing, Sandy Adirondack, 1998 (£14.95)
Voluntary but not Amateur, Duncan Forbes, Ruth Hayes and Jacki Reason, 1998 (£14.95)

Published by Penguin

Managing without Profit, Mike Hudson, 2nd edition 1999 (£12.99)

Other useful publications

Published by the Centre for Voluntary Organisation, London School of Economics (020 7955 7375)

Management Committees: Roles and tasks, Working Paper 4, Margaret Harris, May 1987 (£5.95)

Management Committees in Practice: A study in local voluntary leadership, Working Paper 7, Margaret Harris, April 1989 (£5.95)

Exploring the Role of Voluntary Management Committees: A new approach, Working Paper 10, Margaret Harris, November 1991 (£5.95)

The Only Step in the Line: The lone manager in the small voluntary organisation, Case Study 2, Philip Peatfield, April 1991 (£4.00)

The Power and Authority of Governing Bodies: Three models of practice in service providing agencies, Working Paper 13, Margaret Harris, July 1993 (£5.95)

Trusting and Talking: The relationship between directors and chairs of voluntary agencies, Working Paper 18, John Dowsett and Margaret Harris, November 1996 (£5.95)

A Planned Journey into the Unknown, Working Paper 20, Yogesh Chauhan, October 1998 (£5.95)

Published by Peter Bedford Housing Association (020 7226 6074)
Who Do You Think You're Listening to_?: 25 years of participation, (£4.95)